The Puzzle of Religion

FINDING BELIEFS WE CAN AGREE ON

Douglas Hufschmid

ISBN: 1537681028

ISBN 13: 9781537681023

Library of Congress Control Number: 2016915470

CreateSpace Independent Publishing Platform

North Charleston, South Carolina

Contents

Introduction

Humans have debated whether God exists and life has a higher purpose as far back in history as we can see. Yet after all these debates, atheists are still arguing that God doesn't exist, while believers are still fighting over what God wants, as if we haven't made any progress on these puzzles whatsoever.

Certainly, millions of people claim to understand God and life's purpose, but if we don't have a consensus on religion, then we haven't solved the puzzle of religion. Moreover, until we get a consensus on religion, there is little hope for peace in many parts of our world.

In contrast to the lack of unity supplied by religion, science unites people from all over the world around a universal set of laws. This isn't surprising because science focuses on the experimentally verifiable, while religion must explain the intangible.

Although religion is often simplistic, as a serious pursuit it's actually more challenging than science because God, the afterlife, and any higher purpose to life can't be experimentally verified. Instead, we must rely on logic, intuition, and experience to develop our religious beliefs and decide if the religious beliefs held by others are true.

So how can we understand God and life's purpose? The solution is if God purposely designed our world, then there should be a consistent theme to reality. Moreover, we should be able to figure out what God wants from us by observing what reality does to us on a daily basis.

Of course, most religions and many atheists try to explain God and life's purpose, or lack thereof, by analyzing reality, so this book isn't doing anything new. I'm just trying to offer a more logical and unifying explanation of God and life's purpose.

To make a long story short, let's say there are 2 beliefs in our world: science and religion. In this short story, science says God is neutral or nonexistent while most religions say God and the world are not neutral. Certainly, not all scientists deny God and some Eastern religions do, but my point is that one analysis of reality concludes that the world is neutral while the opposing assessments claim that the world reacts to our karma and/or prayers.

As children, we had to figure out who was correct: those pushing scientism or those pushing a religion. We had to figure out if the world would be neutral to us or if the world would react to our prayers and deeds. Unfortunately, the answer isn't clear because God obviously doesn't answer all our prayers, and yet, the world doesn't seem completely neutral either.

Although a majority of people believe in God, religion is divisive because our religions don't adequately explain the universe. Of course, most people should agree that life is too complex for any mortal to fully understand and explain. This, in fact, is the great human dilemma: we must make sense of a world that we can't fully understand.

Although science can't explain everything, science has made sense of nature by revealing the fundamental laws that govern nature. This is the challenge for religion: reveal the fundamental laws that govern God's behavior.

If karma doesn't right all wrongs, God doesn't answer all our prayers, and life isn't just a neutral chemical reaction either, then what is going on? My suggestion is God is challenging us. My belief is God is our opponent.

Just like our opponent in tennis or chess, God is going to challenge us and make us take action. God is going to hit the ball into our court even though we would like to leave the ball in God's court. This view of God should please those who are tired of the religions that stress thoughts and prayers over action. However, this view of God will annoy those who want God to give them an easy life and those who want to blame Satan for life's challenges.

Many people believe that God is all good and the devil is responsible for all disease, natural disasters, and temptations. In 2017, Pope Francis even suggested changing the Lord's Prayer so it would no longer state that God leads us into temptation. But blaming the devil hasn't helped us cure disease, predict natural disasters, or reduce the lure of life's temptations. Only by seeing life as a solvable puzzle, as opposed to a battle between God and Satan, have we come to understand disease, natural disasters, and temptation.

God doesn't act in mysterious ways. It just mystifies people that God would challenge them. It seems that God should give us everything we want and God should make it easy to do the right thing. Instead, God makes it difficult to do the right thing and get the things we want. Apparently, God wants an ethical life to be a challenge.

It's frustrating that God is challenging us when we just want to be happy and when life's challenges seem to interfere with our happiness. However, research suggest that the pursuit of happiness is often self-centered, unhealthy, and self-defeating, while the pursuit of meaning and purpose are more important for well-being. As Dhruv Khullar, M.D. wrote in the New York Times on January 1, 2018, "Research increasingly suggests that purpose is important for a meaningful life--but also for a healthy life. Doing good, it seems, is better than feeling good."

Dr. Khullar went on to say,

> "Purpose and meaning are connected to what researchers call eudaimonic well-being. This is distinct from, and sometimes inversely related to, happiness (hedonic well-being). One constitutes a deeper, more durable state, while the other is superficial and transient."

According to Roy Baumeister, a social psychologist at Florida State University, "What sets human beings apart from animals is not the pursuit of happiness, which occurs all across the natural world, but the pursuit of meaning, which is unique to humans." Happiness results from the fulfilling of one's immediate desires, which all animals are capable of, but meaning and purpose are long-term intellectual and spiritual pursuits, which only humans seem capable of.

We can say there is a God if life's challenges form a pattern that reveal a higher purpose to life. But, as always, it will be difficult to see the pattern in life's challenges if we don't want to be challenged. Only those looking for emotional, intellectual, and spiritual growth will find continuity in the challenges that so often test our courage, strength, and character.

The traditional religions don't portray God as our opponent for a number of reasons, but the main reason is we naturally want to believe that God is on our side. Another reason is the traditional religions explain our world from the perspective of people who lived thousands of years ago when life was filled with injustice, hardship, and disease and there wasn't much humans could do about injustice, hardship, and disease but dream of Heaven or Nirvana. Today, we know that microbes cause disease, technology can reduce life's hardships, and strengthening our democratic institutions can prevent injustice. Today, we should agree that creation is our challenge, that it's something we can learn about and protect from war, disease, injustice, and ecological collapse, as opposed to being something we must renounce or pray for its Armageddon.

Chapter One

Religion

Polls released by the Gallup Organization in 2016 revealed that 36% of Americans said they went to church each week. According to Gallup, "Self-reported church attendance is also lower than it has been in past decades--although perhaps not as low as might be expected, given the decline in church membership and the increase in the percentage of those with no religious identity."

Although church attendance is declining, 36% of Americans attending church each week is still a significant number. Yet studies by the Evangelical Covenant Church and the Journal for the Scientific Study of Religion reveal that Americans over-report how often they go to church by about 50%. This is known as the "halo-effect," where people over-report socially desirable behavior like voting and church attendance and under-report socially undesirable behavior like drinking.

Americans may overstate how often they go to church because being a churchgoer has been a banner of high morality in America. Yet this desire to put forth a religious facade is in decline as those willing to admit they have no religious affiliation are the fastest growing religious group in America.

Gallup discussed this change in 2016, "The most significant trend in Americans' religiosity in recent decades has been the growing shift away from formal or official religion." In the 1940s, Gallup found that just 2% of Americans were unaffiliated, but they increased to 21% in 2017. Polls by the Pew Research Center found slightly higher numbers, or that 23% of U.S. adults and 35% of Millennials--adults under 30--were unaffiliated in 2014. The Public Religion Research Institute reported that 24% of U.S. adults were unaffiliated in 2016 with some states having even higher numbers. For example, PRRI found that 41% of Vermont residents and about 33% of adults living in Oregon, Washington, Hawaii, Colorado, and New Hampshire were religiously unaffiliated. To put the percentage of unaffiliated adults in perspective, Evangelicals were just 25% of the U.S. population and Catholics were only 21% in 2016.

Numerous studies show that church attendance and religious affiliation has been declining for decades. In fact, the only study to show a gain by religion was a 2010 Gallup poll that found a slight 1% increase in church attendance over the previous two years. However, this small increase in church attendance was linked to the large number of baby boomers who were entering their sixties.

It's thought that as baby boomers enter their sixties, they become more focused on the end of life and, thus, become more interested in the religious discussions about what happens after death than people under sixty. Yet this slight increase in religiosity among Baby Boomers is overshadowed by the large decrease in religiosity among Millennials.

In 2010, the Pew Forum compared the beliefs of present-day 18 to 29-year-olds to the beliefs of earlier generations of 18 to 29-year-olds. They found that young adults were much less religious on a number of key measures than in the past. A 2009 survey by LifeWay Christian Resources also found that a majority of young adults don't pray, don't worship, don't read the Bible, and have increased doubts about traditional Christian beliefs, such as, whether Jesus is the only path to Heaven. In addition, studies by the General Social Survey (GSS) and the National Congregations Study (NCS) taken between 2000 and 2006 revealed that congregations and their clergy are older than in the past. Finally, studies by the Pew Research Center in 2015 found that the average age of evangelical and mainline Christians, (the denominations that contain the most devout churchgoers) is 59, while the median age of the religiously unaffiliated is 36.

These studies might suggest that young people no longer believe in God. But numerous polls show that belief in God has remained fairly constant through the generations at about 90%. What young people have lost is their faith in organized religion.

America is changing and will continue to change because each generation is less attached to the traditional religions than the previous generation. Yet this continual abandonment of the organized religions makes sense when we look at what the traditional religions offer.

First of all, the traditional religions have always offered an explanation of our universe. At one time, religion offered the only explanation of how life arose, the movement of the sun and stars, and what causes the weather and our illnesses. But unless children are home-schooled or in strict religious schools, they learn from science about life's creation, the movement of the sun and stars, and what causes the weather and their ailments.

For most young people, religion explains only what science can't explain. But studies released by the Barna Group in 2011 show that even young Christians are losing interest in what their religion is explaining, causing, "59% to disconnect either permanently or for an extended period of time from church life after age 15." Barna also reported that, "31% of 18 to 29-year-old Christians said church is boring and out of step with their life, 25% said Bible teaching is unclear and just demonizes everything outside of church, 35% said Christians are too confident they know all the answers, 29% feel churches are out of step with the scientific world they live in, and 23% said they have been turned off by the creation-versus-evolution debate."

This study of why young Christians are leaving the church also found that:

> "A few of the defining characteristics of today's teens and young adults are their unprecedented access to ideas and worldviews as well as their prodigious consumption of popular culture. As Christians, they express the desire for their faith in Christ to connect to the world they live in. However, much of their experience of Christianity feels stifling, fear-based and risk-averse.

Young adults with Christian experience say the church is not a place that allows them to express doubts. They do not feel safe admitting that sometimes Christianity does not make sense. In addition, many feel that the church's response to doubt is trivial. Some of the perceptions in this regard include not being able "to ask my most pressing life questions in church" (36%) and having "significant intellectual doubts about my faith" (23%). In a related theme of how churches struggle to help young adults who feel marginalized, about one out of every six young adults with a Christian background said their faith "does not help with depression or other emotional problems" they experience (18%)."

Christianity is failing young people more than adults. The above polls reveal a number of reasons for this, but the main reason is Christianity just tells simple, idealized stories that don't mesh with the complex world that young people live in. For example, Christianity tells young people that sex before marriage is a sin. Although it might be ideal to have only one sex partner, it's simplistic when we reach puberty by age 13 and the average age people first marry is 27.4 years for women and 29.5 years for men in 2017.

What's the purpose of having humans go through puberty by age 13 when most people won't marry until their late twenties? That isn't intelligent design, unless you believe that God wants to challenge young people, their parents, and everyone else in society who has to deal with teenagers and their raging hormones.

Of course, science and evolution can explain the intelligence of having teenage parents. But many Christians deny evolution and, instead, tell another simple, idealized story: that life was created in 6 days.

Elderly people whose life is behind them may not care that, "sometimes Christianity does not make sense," but young people who are trying to understand the life that stretches out before them want beliefs that make sense. Moreover, as our knowledge of the universe advances, people of all ages are tiring of the simplistic stories put forth by religion. That's why, according to Pew in 2015, "It's not just millennials leaving the church. Whether married or single, rich or poor, young or old, living in the West or the Bible Belt, almost every demographic group has seen a significant drop in people who call themselves Christians."

Another reason why religion was more popular in the past is child-labor and death from infectious diseases was rampant just 100 years ago. Those hardships made it easier for both the young and old to relate to religious stories that so often focus on death, suffering, and the end-times. But today, science has cured most of the infectious diseases that plagued humanity and few young people experience child labor. Today, most people see life as fun and religion as dreary and out-of-date.

Besides losing ground to science, most religions have also lost the moral high-ground. For example, surveys by PRRI in 2014, Gallup in 2012, General Social Survey in 2015, and the Pew Research Center in 2015 show that most young people now accept many of the behaviors that the traditional religions consider immoral, such as: the use of birth control, sex before marriage, and interfaith, interracial, and same-sex relations. Furthermore, the incessant child-sex-abuse scandals have convinced people of all ages that the organized religions have lost their moral authority.

Of course, most religions also explain God. Yet by failing to convince young people that they understand the natural world, modern times, and morality, the organized religions have failed to convince young people that they understand God.

Besides offering knowledge, most religions also offer a community. And there is no denying that people need communities and that going to a house of worship is a good way to network. More importantly, being part of a religious community was often the only way to network in the not too distant past.

Before phones, cars, and the internet, or just 100 years ago in most parts of America, the only way to connect with friends, relatives, and business associates was by foot or horseback. Sounds romantic but walking or riding a horse for more than a few miles can be an enormous challenge, especially in bad weather and after a day of hard work. This is another reason why religion was so popular in the past: each house of worship offered a central location and prescribed times where everyone could meet.

Although people also went to markets and taverns to socialize, the only time and place where you could be sure that people from all over the countryside would come together were the weekly congregations compelled by religious worship and prayer. This made going to church enjoyable for the young and the old, the married and the single, the pious and the nonreligious because it was the most reliable way to connect with friends, relatives, romantic interests, business associates, and so on.

The weekly church services also made going to church the most practical way to check up on the health and wellbeing of people who lived more than a short walk away. But in today's world, few people need a church to connect with others. Today, people can join communities that reflect their modern social, moral, and intellectual beliefs.

Another practical reason to go to church is the social safety-net that most religious communities offer. However, as poverty has declined and the government has increasingly provided financial aid, another historically important reason to join a religion has faded away.

A purely cultural reason to go to church is the music, literature, and spectacle that most religious services offer. But the music, fables, and pageantry in our traditional places of worship now pale in comparison to modern concerts, movies, television shows, video games, theme parks, and sporting events, so in yet another area once dominated by religion, religion is seen as antiquated, especially by young people.

Lastly, most religions offer salvation. And many churchgoers will argue that this is the most important part of religion and that all the above are just added benefits of going to church. But, as with everything else religion is offering, the promise that one particular religion has the exclusive path to Heaven isn't bringing young people back to church.

In the small towns where our ancestors used to live, there was usually only one religion and little way for the average, illiterate person to learn of other religions. This made the claims of each religion seem unique. Yet most young people now live in large cities or sprawling urban areas and are exposed to so many different religions each claiming to be the only path to Heaven that this claim has also grown old.

It wasn't long ago that religion was the best, if not the only source for knowledge, morality, community, welfare, and entertainment. Yet the only thing that religion now excels at is tradition and the simple fables, simple interactions, and simple entertainment that come from a simpler time. Obviously, the older a person is, the more they will enjoy these old-time offerings. But if the world's religions have nothing to offer the younger generations but the past, then they will continue to fade away into the past.

To stay relevant, many churches are trying to update their beliefs, entertainment, and social interactions. The mega-churches have done this best with their positive theologies, rock music, and internet cafes. These modernizations have allowed the mega-churches to grow over 8% per year according to research by Hartford Seminary in 2011 while overall church attendance has declined 20% according to Barna research.

Mega-churches are not your typical corner church. They are huge, mall-like structures with acres of parking that impact the community like a modest-size retail center. Studies by the Hartford Institute for Religion Research reveal that the eight most popular mega-churches have over 20,000 people attending each week, while the next 50 most popular have between 10,000 and 20,000 people attending weekly. This is one of the main attractions of the mega-churches: they offer a readymade, super-sized community to join.

The mega-church sanctuary is also thoroughly modern with stadium seating and state of the art sound and projection systems. These massive auditoriums seat about 1,500 people on average with the larger sanctuaries seating between 5,000 and 10,000 people. In contrast, the average movie theater seats between 200 and 300 people.

Adjacent to the mega-church sanctuary is usually a gym, bookstore, and internet café, which makes these churches a sort of all-inclusive-resort. This hasn't gone unnoticed, and some states, like Tennessee have gone to court arguing that gyms, bookstores, and cafés are "commercial enterprises" that should be taxed.

Mega-church worshipers also reflect modern society by being about 40 years old on average, which is similar to the 2010 U.S. census average of 36.8 years old. In contrast, the traditional churchgoer is about 53 years old on average. Lastly, mega-church worshipers are more diverse in race and marital status and have higher income and education levels than traditional churchgoers.

The mega-churches are attracting a younger, more diverse, and more affluent crowd than the traditional churches. This might lead one to believe that mega-churches are bringing people back to religion. But pastors of many smaller churches, like Randy Hammer, a pastor at the 100-member Grace Cumberland Presbyterian Church, complain that mega-churches are just stealing their members. If anything, the mega-churches may be slowing the decline of church attendance by attracting those young people who would have abandoned the traditional churches.

Traditional churchgoers have other complaints about the mega-churches besides their stealing of disciples. Some complain about the blaring rock music, big screen TVs, and shorts and flip-flops worn by the young attendees. Others say that mega-church worshipers are mostly spectators because studies show that 45% never volunteer at church and 32% donate little or no money to the mega-church. Another complaint is that mega-church theology is a generic, hybrid Christianity. Many critics say it just, "church lite," or two miles long and one-inch deep. There is also denigration of the prosperity theology emphasized in mega-churches like Joel Osteen's and the feel-good, motivational self-help offered in mega-churches like those run by Rick Warren. Yet these more relaxed and upbeat theologies may be another reason why the mega-churches are gaining members while the traditional churches are losing members: many people prefer church services that are informal and emotional rather than analytical and theological.

Although it's easy to condemn the mega-churches for being superficial, most churchgoers may not want their intellect challenged in church. This was revealed in a 2007 Gallup poll of people who attended church regularly. This poll found that only 23% of people who attend church monthly said they were looking for "spiritual growth," while all the other reasons given for attending church were less introspective. For example, 20% of respondents said that they attend church because church keeps them "grounded/inspired," 15% said "it's my faith," another 15% went to church to "worship God," 13% attended for "the fellowship of other members/the community," 12% were fulfilling a "family tradition," and the remaining 12% said they went to church because they "believe in God/ believe in religion."

If most people went to church for spiritual growth, then the traditional, new age, and mega-churches would offer more intellectually challenging services. But most people go to church for inspiration, faith, worship, fellowship, tradition, and belief, so if a church is to be successful, it must cater to those less reflective desires.

A substantial challenge for church leaders and anyone trying to understand religion is that people go to church for varied and fluctuating reasons. This makes it difficult to understand what religion is and what church should offer because there isn't a single or a constant reason that people go to church. This also makes it difficult to turn religion into a unifying branch of knowledge because only a minority of people have a true passion for spiritual knowledge.

A 2012 study by the University of Washington revealed another reason why the mega-churches are growing why the traditional churches are declining: emotion and large group experiences have been shown to raise levels of oxytocin in humans. Oxytocin is often called the "love hormone" because it stimulates pair bonding and maternal behavior. The dark side is it also encourages tribal behavior by stimulating trust and empathy with the in-group and suspicion and rejection of outsiders.

Like the producers of rock concerts and sporting events, many mega-church pastors have also learned to use music, visual images, and audience participation to create a sense of euphoria in the crowd. Yet the euphoria created in church is often seen as a connection with the divine, even though it's probably just another oxytocin-induced pleasure--a pleasure that most animals need to facilitate social bonding.

It's clear to those who study religion that the mega-churches have prospered by using the latest technology, market research, and opinion polls to update the social, entertainment, and even the theological aspects of religion. But should religion be just a market-driven, euphoria-inducing, social event, or should it be the best explanation of God and morality that we can attain?

So here is this book's main puzzle: "What is religion?" And I'm not asking for a historical description of Christianity, Buddhism, Hinduism, and so on. I'm asking if religion is an advancing branch of knowledge, or just an entertaining, social event.

Of course, religion can be a branch of knowledge and an entertaining social event because education can be fun for the whole family, especially when a little fantasy is mixed in. But mixing education and entertainment is difficult because entertaining people and educating people are often conflicting endeavors. The reason is many parts of life are complex while many other parts are upsetting to learn about.

If you want to entertain people, then it's best to divert them away from the complex and unpleasant parts of reality. But if your goal is to educate people, then you must discuss the complex and unpleasant parts of reality. If you try to do both, then you won't do as well at either. That's one reason why religion is losing ground to science and Hollywood.

Science offers the most cutting-edge knowledge without concern for being entertaining. Hollywood offers the most advanced entertainment without worrying about being educational. Religion tries to compete by offering simpler knowledge and more old-fashioned entertainment. But religion is losing the competition for young minds because its simpler knowledge and old-fashioned entertainment isn't impressing young people enough to steer them away from science and Hollywood. Instead, polls by Gallup show that young adults are more accepting of scientific theories like evolution and polls by the Pew Research Center show that young adults are less concerned about Hollywood threatening their values than older adults.

People who want the most advanced knowledge turn to science. People who want the most advanced entertainment turn to Hollywood. And those who want the simple fables and old-fashioned entertainment offered by the traditional religions are a shrinking segment of society.

Even in the areas of life that only religion is supposed to be capable of explaining, such as: what happens after death, scientists are competing by investigating what happens at the moment of death. Moreover, the medical investigations of near-death and out-of-body experiences are often more nuanced and thought-provoking than the traditional religious discussions of Heaven and Hell.

Scientists have invaded so much of religion's territory to offer their own explanations for how life arose, how old the Earth is, and which behaviors are normal and healthy that religion no longer retains the exclusive rights to explain any part of life. At this point, religion just owns the simple, traditional explanations of life, while science owns the modern, complex, and evidence-based explanations of life.

Perhaps the last argument for the continued importance of the traditional religions is that revelation and faith offer different ways of understanding our world than reason and evidence. Certainly, science can't explain everything, but revelation and faith aren't offering new insights into our universe. Again, this is the problem with most organized religions: they cling to the past and resist new ideas.

The battle between science and religion isn't over methodology; it's just between simple, traditional beliefs and modern, complex, evidence-based beliefs. For example, the battle between the Catholic Church and Galileo wasn't over Galileo's methods because the inquisition refused to even look at Galileo's evidence. The battle was just between the simple, traditional story that everything revolves around the Earth and the more complex and modern evidence that the Earth is just one of many planets orbiting our sun. Similarly, the ongoing battle between creationism and evolution isn't about Darwin's methods; it's just between the simple, traditional story that life was created in six days and the more complex and modern evidence that life evolves through generational variations and natural selection.

We can excuse the world's religions for offering simplistic stories because they're such ancient forms of knowledge. What's inexcusable is many religions resist new, evidence-based ideas because they want to be seen as complete and infallible knowledge that no one can question or compete with.

Claiming that any religion is the inerrant word of God is just another simple story that competes with the evidence. For example, any rational examination of the Bible reveals that it contains too many inaccuracies, contradictions, and justifications for slavery, genocide, and stoning people to death to be the inerrant wisdom of God.

Obviously, many edicts in the Bible have no place in modern society. This should be proof that the Bible is just the beliefs of people who lived thousands of years ago. Yet even though few people alive today would consider obeying many of the laws and advice in the Bible, about 24% of adults in 2017 said that the Bible is the literal word of God. This is the lowest percent in Gallup's 40-year polling.

As with all other religious beliefs, the belief that the Bible is the literal word of God has decreased most among young adults: decreasing from 32% in 1976 to just 12% in 2017. Also not surprising, the belief that the Bible is infallible rises and falls with education, rising to 31% for those with just a high school education and falling to 13% for those with a college degree.

Clearly, education helps people understand that God hasn't given anyone all the answers. That's why our best hope for turning religion into an advancing branch of knowledge is to expand everyone's understanding of our world.

Chapter Two

Learning

Education is the solution to most of our problems. And educating people might sound easy. Unfortunately, many people shy away from difficult mental challenges just as many shy away from difficult physical challenges.

Stuart Shanker, Professor Emeritus of philosophy and psychology at York University, wrote in 2017 for Psychology Today, "concentration demands an awful lot of energy, which is why the heart starts pumping. We grit our teeth, clench our jaws, scrunch our foreheads, squeeze our core muscles, breathe more rapidly, start to sweat; and meanwhile, digestion and metabolic processes slow down. In other words, when we concentrate we go into what Ernst Gellhorn called an "ergotropic" state, which was originally designed for hunting and survival, but which we put to use today for figuring out our taxes." When we face problems that overload our brain, "The limbic system serves as a non-cognitive brake on the rational brain. The hypothalamus operates like a thermostat, shutting down an energy-consuming activity when blood glucose levels drop below a threshold."

Perhaps this is why it's so difficult to engage people in complex discussions: their hypothalamus will shut-down their brain when they are bombarded them with too many complicated thoughts.

Before we can advance our religious beliefs, we must understand why people are driven away from complex beliefs. We must acknowledge that our brain is a muscle that is limited and constrained just like all our other muscles are limited and constrained, which can make people mentally lazy. As Claude Messier of the University of Ottawa wrote in Scientific American in 2012, "My general hypothesis is that the brain is a lazy bum.

The brain has a hard time staying focused on just one thing for too long. It's possible that sustained concentration creates some changes in the brain that promote avoidance of that state. It could be like a timer that says, 'Okay you're done now.' Maybe the brain just doesn't like to work so hard for so long."

It's logical, even intuitive that thinking is strenuous and that many people would want to avoid complex thoughts just as many people want to avoid strenuous exercise. But calling people lazy raises another dilemma. As Neel Burton M.D. wrote in 2015, "the very concept of laziness presupposes the ability to choose not to be lazy—that is, presupposes the existence of free will."

Before we can discuss any of the forces that cause people to have different beliefs, we must keep in mind that science is unable to verify if we have a conscious self with free will to choose between different beliefs. As far as science can tell, everything we do and believe is predetermined. Joachim I. Krueger, Professor of Psychology at Brown University, wrote in 2013 that psychologists "have to choose between doing science and believing in free will; they could not have a science of free will."

The contradiction between free will and determinism has been discussed since the early Greeks, and we still lack a unifying solution. However, most people (70%) believe in free will. More importantly, believing in free will seems to affect our behavior, both increasing our motivation and making us more judgmental.

According to a 2017 study detailed in Frontiers in Psychology, entitled The Influence of (Dis)belief in Free Will on Immoral Behavior, by Emilie A. Caspar, Laurène Vuillaume, Pedro A. Magalhães De Saldanha da Gama, and Axel Cleeremans,

> "a substantial body of scientific research has highlighted the prosocial benefits of believing in free will, as well as the negative effects of denying its existence (e.g., Wegner, 2002; Vohs and Schooler, 2008; Baumeister et al., 2009; Leotti et al., 2010; Stillman et al., 2010). For instance, Baumeister et al. (2009) suggested that people who believe

in free will exhibit a higher prosocial and altruistic behavior, and Vohs and Schooler (2008) observed that participants who were primed with disbelief in free will cheated more often than a group of control participants. According to Baumeister (2008), believing in free will increases one's motivation and willingness to make efforts, therefore resulting in higher self-control. This argument has been supported by recent electroencephalography studies showing that inducing disbelief in free will changes the neural processes underlying voluntary action (Rigoni et al., 2011) and post error adaptation (Rigoni et al., 2013, 2015). Nonetheless, these "pro free will" arguments remain quite controversial (Miles, 2013). Some studies have indicated that believing in determinism may also have positive effects (Westlake and Paulhus, 2007; Krueger et al., 2014; Shariff et al., 2014). For instance, Shariff et al. (2014) showed that people who believe in determinism exhibit reduced retributive attitudes toward others. Congruently, Krueger et al. (2014) showed that people who strongly believe in free will tend to be more punitive. In the same line of thought, Westlake and Paulhus (2007) observed that people who scored high on free will tended to assign more severe sentences to offenders. Our results show that participants who were primed with a text defending neural determinism – the idea that humans are a mere bunch of neurons guided by their biology – administered fewer shocks and were less vindictive toward the other participant. Importantly, this finding only held for female participants. These results show the complex interaction between gender, (dis)beliefs in free will and moral behavior.

According to the above authors, "Beliefs in free will and determinism can have positive impacts on moral-decision makings." But the question remains, "How could belief in free will change our behavior if we lack the free will to change our behavior?" Unfortunately, science has no way to explain how an intangible belief could alter the course of our physical body.

Atheists often say, "I will believe in God when there is proof of God." Sounds noble, but we need to decide today if God exists because we need to make moral decisions today. Similarly, we can't wait for proof of free will because we need to make judgements today about our choices and the choices of others. As mentioned in the introduction, the great human dilemma is we have to live in the absence of proof of God, free will, the afterlife, and so on. Our only choice is to do what's most logical. And Einstein's response was, "I am a determinist," but, "I am compelled to act as if free will existed because if I wish to live in a civilized society I must act responsibly."

If life is predetermined, then we can have a purely scientific discussion of our beliefs and behaviors. But if God and we can alter our destiny, then we cannot expect science to fully explain life. Instead, those who want to live in a civilized society must use science and logic to understand and make judgements about our beliefs and behaviors.

To discuss free will isn't to ignore science; it's to go beyond science. It's to know where science ends and philosophy begins. It's to use science to explain how physical and biological forces drive our behavior and to use logic to explain how our mind might motivate us to battle against those physical and biological forces.

Although free will is unscientific, free will would not lead to illogical behaviors because physical and biological forces would still constrain our bodies. To put it another way: we can't defy the laws of physics; we can only choose how to expend our limited energy. The question for logic is, "Why do different people choose to expend their limited energy in different ways?"

Science can explain why certain behaviors require more energy than other behaviors and why people strive for the least energy consuming behaviors whenever possible. The unscientific part is theorizing why some people choose more energy expensive behaviors than other people when there is no evolutionary benefit to those more strenuous behaviors.

Science can also explain why our thoughts require electrical signals and chemical reactions to occur within our brain, why these electrical signals and chemical reactions require energy, and why humans have a limited ability to replenish their energy. The unscientific part is theorizing why some people choose more energy expensive beliefs than other people when there is no evolutionary benefit to possessing those more complicated beliefs. The final challenge is figuring out how we can encourage people to spend more energy on their beliefs and behaviors so they can live more fulfilling lives and we can build stronger societies.

Because the human brain uses about 20% of our resting energy, it makes sense that people would resist turning on such a costly organ and that people would get tired and fatigued after extended thinking. And studies have shown that people make better decisions early in the day and after a meal when they are not low on energy. A study in 2014 at Brigham and Women's Hospital revealed that physicians prescribe 5% more unnecessary antibiotics as they fatigue during their morning and afternoon appointments. In 2011, researchers at Ben-Gurion University (Israel) found that judges hand out harsher sentences later in the day, or that 70 percent of prisoners who appeared early in the morning received parole, while only 10 percent of those who appeared late in the day were paroled. Francesca Gino, Tandon Family Professor of Business Administration at Harvard Business School, Hans Henrik Sievertsen of the Danish National Centre for Social Research, and Marco Piovesan of the University of Copenhagen analyzed the complete test data on the full population of 8 to 15-year-old children in Danish public schools from 2009/10 and 2012/13 to reveal that the later in the day the time of the test was, the lower was the students' performance on the test. Finally, a study published in the Journal of Applied Physiology in March of 2009 found that people who perform complex mental tasks tire more quickly when put on an exercise bike than people who were mentally rested. These studies all show that thinking is not an effortless endeavor and that humans cannot engage in extended mental exertion without tangible and, often, negative repercussions.

If we experience stress and fatigue when thinking, then we will not engage in rigorous thought without trepidation. Instead, many people will avoid complex thoughts just as many people avoid strenuous exercises.

Although it makes sense that humans can't think effortlessly and endlessly, our brain doesn't use significantly more energy when it's active than when it's resting, so something else must be adding to the strain. What scientists have found is that exerting our brain in ways that we don't find enjoyable elicits a stress response and it's this stress response that truly makes our thought process so taxing. For example, a 2008 study comparing Canadian students who either sat around, summarized a passage of text, or completed a series of computerized attention and memory tests for 45 minutes found that the students whose brains were busy had significantly more of the stress hormone *cortisol* in their bloodstream and their heart rates, blood pressure, and anxiety levels were higher than the students who just sat around.

Could our desire to conserve energy and avoid stress cause some people to prefer the simple stories of religion over the complex theories of science? Moreover, could our desire to conserve energy and avoid stress cause other people to believe in atheism and determinism? The logical answer is yes because the most challenging world is one where science, free will, and God must all be understood. The thoughts demanded by this world can be undesirable because their strenuousness can cause the release of the stress hormone *cortisol*. This hormone stimulates the "fight or flight response," which quickens our heart rate, causes us to sweat, and makes us fidgety. This is not only uncomfortable, but it's also exhausting.

A purely material world is simpler than a world overseen by God. Similarly, people who lack free will are easier to understand than people who have a conscious self with the ability to make choices. But we may need to understand the most complex world where science, God, and free will all coexist.

If people have free will, then it's logical that many people would choose simple beliefs to avoid exerting their brain just as many people choose easy exercises to avoid exerting their body. Of course, there are also social and economic forces driving people to choose the traditional, new age, or atheistic explanations of life over more complex explanations of life and we will discuss all those reasons in the following chapters. Yet the first and most fundamental reason why many people prefer simple, one-dimensional beliefs is they are less strenuous than more complicated beliefs.

Releasing cortisol when the brain is exerted makes sense from an evolutionary standpoint because, in the distant past, a highly active brain wouldn't occur just because our ancestors were thinking about God, the afterlife, and free will. It would occur because our ancestors were in real danger. It would occur when our ancestors were confronting life or death situations, like a pride of lions, some enemy warriors, or a narrow path along a cliff. These were the mental challenges that our ancestors encountered on a regular basis and it makes sense that those who were put on high alert would get out of these situations better than those who weren't. Unfortunately, cortisol now drives people to avoid or quickly get out of mental challenges that aren't life threating.

The dangers and hardships of the ancient world have largely disappeared. However, many people still experience what they feel is too much stress and fatigue from problems at work and home. The modern stresses of making a living and maintaining relationships drive some people away from the additional stress of contemplating life's great religious questions like, "How could the universe arise from nothing" and "What happens after death?"

Trying to figure out how the universe arose from nothing and what happens after death can cause as much stress and anxiety as trying to escape from a dangerous predator. In each situation, there are no simple answers, only a flood of cortisol makes people want to fight or get away.

This is why so many people feel that the simple answers of religion are worth fighting for: they offer relief from the stress of contemplating life's big questions. This is also why Galileo and Darwin were unable to change the established beliefs even though they had evidence for their beliefs: few people wanted to struggle with Galileo and Darwin's more complex answers when religion was already offering simple answers.

Religious convictions allow people to avoid the stress of additional inquiry. Of course, atheism and scientism also supply complete answers to a universe that we cannot fully explain. Moreover, apathy and extreme political ideologies also allow people to reduce their thoughts.

Again, the human dilemma is we can't fully explain life. This isn't a problem for those who enjoy complicated puzzles, but it stresses-out those who want simple answers.

The complexity and mystery of life causes many people to seek out simple answers and the charlatans who provide them. It causes many people to gravitated towards preachers and politicians who spout non-sense or outright lies because reality is so inexplicable.

The selling of simple answers is a lucrative business regardless of how absurd those answers are and regardless of whether the answers are tied to science or religion, atheism or theism, conservatism or liberalism. More troubling is that even after a charlatan is exposed, people still trust and revere them because they know that a proven charlatan will never trouble them with the truth or burden them with complicated answers. That's why, Peter Popoff, who was exposed as a charlatan by James Randi for using an earpiece to receive radio messages from his wife giving him the home addresses and ailments of audience members which he purported had come from God during faith healing rallies in 1986 went bankrupt the next year but was able to rebuild his ministries and was collecting over $9.6 million in 2003 and over $23 million 2005, according to Wikipedia.

As children, we are told not to lie. As adults, we discover that few people want to hear the truth. We discover that the more our preach-ers and politicians lie, the more some people trust them. We discover that those who tell the truth have, throughout history, been push aside or persecuted.

We are united by our inability to fully explain life. Unfortunately, we are divided by all the people who crave simple answers and all the charlatans who cater to them.

The intelligent solution to living in our infinitely complex universe is to keep our mind open and avoid embracing simple answers. Unfortunately, that takes more energy and emotional fortitude than many people feel they have.

Chapter Three

Objectivity

It would be easier to advance our beliefs if humans were objective machines that accepted information without complaint. Unfortunately, people often object to the knowledge they are given, such as, whether vaccines are safe and climate change is manmade. This makes it seem like humans are irrational. Yet the rational is people avoid those beliefs that require too much mental and emotional work. The rational is we are not machines; we are biological organisms who are driven to conserve energy and avoid stress.

Experiments in 2015 by Troy Campbell, assistant professor of marketing at the University of Oregon and Justin Friesen, assistant professor of psychology at the University of Winnipeg found that, "when people's beliefs are threatened, they often take flight to a land where facts do not matter." Confirmation bias allows people to keep their beliefs static and stay within their group, as opposed to continually revving up their brains, rethinking their beliefs, and, perhaps, leaving one's religious or political group.

Reality is difficult for everyone to understand and accept. That's why the goal of psychotherapy is to help everyone cope with our complex and often stressful world. Perhaps religion is just an ancient form of psychotherapy because it uses simple stories to help people cope with the complex and unpleasant parts of life. The problem is we need to move beyond the simple fables of religion because they aren't helping us cope with the complex issues of war, environmental degradation, and overpopulation. Unfortunately, moving beyond our traditional religions is difficult when alternative explanations of life are more complicated, incomplete, and less engrained in our families and communities.

A primary goal of religion is to offer a simple, complete, and comforting explanation of our universe. Yet the primary goal of science is to offer an accurate explanation of our universe. Moreover, the disparity in these goals is amplified by the fact that the income of scientists is dependent on the accuracy of the medicines and technologies they develop, whereas religion isn't producing anything physical, but has only its stories to sell.

Selling medicines and technologies is different than selling stories because the former must be accurate or people will stop buying them, while the latter can be pure fantasy and people will continue buying them. This doesn't mean that religious stories can't offer wisdom, but that the main goal in storytelling is to divert people away from our complex and challenging world, whereas the primary goal and entire financial incentive in science is to accurately describe our complicated universe.

Luckily, people are becoming more comfortable with the complex theories of science because of all the medicines and technologies produced by science and because each generation is exposed to science at a younger age, which makes science less overwhelming. At this point, people are growing tired of the simple stories offered by religion. Yet no matter how comfortable people become with science, religion will always exist because science can't explain everything.

Science can't eliminate religion because science can't verify if there is a God, an afterlife, or a higher purpose to life. To explain things that we can't experimentally verify, we will have to rely on what philosophers have always relied on--logic. We may also have to accept that some things, like the afterlife, may always exist beyond our comprehension.

It's naïve to expect science to answer all our questions. However, logic and reason can produce some open, evidence-based explanations of God and life's purpose to compete with all the closed, faith-based claims of religion.

As mentioned in the introduction, if God purposely designed our world, then we should be able to develop some logical assumptions about God by studying the design of creation. To put it another way, by analyzing what reality does to us, we should be able to determine what God wants from us.

If we discover that reality is consistently and universally doing something to all of us, then this should be evidence of God's intention. Again, my suggestion is God is challenging us to encourage our emotional, spiritual, and intellectual growth. Unfortunately, most people won't see this pattern in life's challenges because most people aren't looking for emotional, spiritual, and intellectual growth. Most people are looking for happiness, or an easy life devoid of challenges, and so they are frustrated and confused when life keeps challenging them.

Although many religions claim to encourage emotional, spiritual, and intellectual growth, many also resist any further explanations of God, the natural world, and life's purpose, which discourages such growth. Many religions just tell simple, entertaining stories because this makes it easy for people to patronize the religion.

The challenge of advancing religion is to open up all the simplistic and infallible beliefs to further scrutiny. But that won't be easy because it requires both the congregation and the religious authorities to consider new and more complicated beliefs, which isn't a desirable situation on either side of the pews.

An ongoing battle between science and many religions pits the simple story that homosexuality is a choice or a mental disorder against the more complex and modern evidence that homosexuality is caused by genes and hormonal events during pregnancy. Of course, it wasn't until 1987 that the American Psychiatric Association declassified homosexuality as a mental illness, so the denial of life's complex and diverse nature isn't just about religion; it's about human nature. In that sense, this book really isn't about religion; it's about human nature, or it's about the forces that cause people to deny life's complexity.

As with past denials of the scientific evidence from Galileo and Darwin, the continual denial of the evidence on homosexuality by certain religious groups is also driven more by an emotional preference for simple stories than any honest dispute with the evidence. It's driven by the desire to inhabit a simple society with only one race, one gender, and one religion.

The more races, genders, and beliefs in the room, the more complex the story and the more emotional and intellectual upheaval is produced. Of course, research shows that liberals are better at handling such novelty while conservatives become anxious in complicated situations.

Emily Laber-Warren explained it this way in Scienctific American Mind on September 1, 2012, "Psychologists have found that conservatives are fundamentally more anxious than liberals, which may be why they typically desire stability, structure and clear answers even to complicated questions."

Many conservative religions denounce homosexuality, not because they have evidence that humans are choosing their sexual orientation, but because of the simple, idealized story that God created men and women to marry for life and have sex only for reproduction. Obviously, homosexuals complicate this story, as does divorce, birth control, masturbation, and premarital sex.

Certainly, we could discuss the individual scriptures that condemn homosexuality, divorce, birth control, masturbation, and premarital sex, but that would give credence to the idea that religion created these taboos. My contention is that human nature creates the desire for simple stories and it's our innate desire to avoid stressing our emotions and intellect that creates the simplistic scriptures.

God doesn't tell simple stories. But people like to hear simple stories, so scripture is written and/or interpreted to conform to the desires of those who put money in the collection plate.

The condemnation of homosexuality, divorce, birth control, masturbation, and premarital sex isn't motivated primarily by scripture; it's motivated primarily by our desire for simple thoughts and emotions. This is why it's becoming difficult to condemn homosexuality, divorce, birth control, masturbation, and premarital sex: humanity is maturing and becoming more liberal.

A majority of people now accept homosexuality, divorce, birth control, masturbation, and premarital sex, but this isn't because the scriptures have changed. It's because people have changed. It's because more people are losing their fear of complicated stories.

Unfortunately, many conservative religions still feel they can condemn homosexuality and exclude homosexuals from their story of life because homosexuals make up such a small percent of the population. Unfortunately, many people are still uncomfortable with the thoughts and emotions that arise from thinking about and encountering homosexuals. Luckily, homosexuals are gaining support from the courts and from the large number of heterosexuals who are tired of the juvenile prejudices spread by the traditional religions.

One of the main factors that young people cite for abandoning religion is the simplistic and outdated beliefs about sexuality spread by the organized religions. According to PRRI, the third most stated reason that all Americans leave their childhood religion is the "negative religious teachings about or treatment of gay and lesbian people (29%)." This means that the world's religions will have to embrace more complex beliefs about human sexuality if they want to remain appealing. Yet the fear of many religions is they won't receive enough donations if they offer more nuanced beliefs about sexuality. The fear is that stirring-up people's emotions over hot-button issues like abortion and homosexuality will always be more lucrative than helping people understand the evidence linking birth control to lower abortion rates and the evidence showing that humans don't choose their sexual orientation. The justifiable fear is that rational people won't give as much money to a church as emotionally aroused people.

Instead of helping people understand our complex and challenging world, many religions do the opposite and prey on the people who are unable to cope with the complex issues of death, sexuality, family planning, and so on. Unfortunately, many religions feel it's more profitable to push people's emotional buttons than to encourage rational thought. Hopefully, this will change as humanity matures.

In 1997, the American Psychological Association (APA) passed a resolution affirming that, "homosexuality is not a mental disorder and that the APA opposes all portrayals of lesbian, gay, and bisexual people as mentally ill and in need of treatment due to their sexual orientation." Unfortunately, this scientific consensus wasn't immediately accepted by the general population. Instead, public opinion remained against same-sex relations for another 15 years.

Scientific evidence doesn't immediately change public opinion because humans do not easily accept new and more complex beliefs. What ultimately changed public opinion about same-sex relations was the fact that more people started to become aware that they were interacting with homosexuals on a daily basis. This was revealed in a 2009, USA Today/Gallup poll that showed how knowing someone who is gay makes people more accepting of same-sex marriage.

The scientific evidence about homosexuality didn't immediately change public opinion about same-sex marriage because a majority of Americans denied knowing anyone in their immediate circle who was gay when the scientific evidence about homosexuality first came out. It wasn't until 2012 that a majority of Americans came to accept same-sex relations. Not surprising, a 2012 CNN/ORC poll revealed that 60% of Americans then admitted to having a family member or close friend who was gay or lesbian. That was up from 49% just two years earlier when public opinion was evenly split on the acceptance of same-sex relations.

Having gay friends and relatives alters the battle between science and religion because it changes the dynamics of what is easy and difficult in both an emotional and intellectual sense. For example, having gay friends and relatives makes it easier intellectually to verify the evidence that homosexuality is not a choice or a mental disorder. Furthermore, having gay friends and relatives makes it emotionally more difficult to be intolerant because you must be intolerant of your own friends and relatives. Lastly, having gay friends and relatives seems to desensitize people to their innate phobias about homosexuality.

Many things in life are mentally and emotionally challenging to learn about and get accustomed to. That's why most people need time and social support to accept new and more complicated beliefs. Hopefully, we will have enough time and social support to accept the scientific consensus on global warming before we cook our environment.

In both religious and secular matters, people are torn between the simple stories and the more complex evidence. That's why our challenge is to help those who are overwhelmed by life's complexity. Our challenge is to create a society where complex answers are encouraged and simple answers are discouraged.

Chapter Four

Unity

In 2007, the Pew Research Center conducted the largest survey of global public opinion ever taken. They asked people from Russia to South Africa and from Canada to Argentina to decide which of five problems posed the greatest threat to our world. The choices were: the spread of nuclear weapons, religious and ethnic hatred, AIDS and other infectious diseases, pollution and other environmental problems, and the growing gap between rich and poor.

The poll revealed that Americans and those in the Middle East felt that nuclear proliferation and religious and ethnic hatred were the greatest threats, while those in Asia saw pollution as the greatest problem. On the African continent, AIDS and other infectious diseases were of greatest concern, while the growing gap between rich and poor caused the most anxiety in countries as diverse as Kenya, Chile, and South Korea.

This survey might lead one to believe that our world's greatest problem depends on where you live. But this overlooks a more universal problem, how our religious and political divisions either create or keep us from solving all the above problems. For example, if our world wasn't religiously divided, then our world wouldn't be plagued by religious hatred. Moreover, if our world wasn't politically divided, then nuclear proliferation wouldn't be so threatening. Finally, if our world wasn't religiously and politically divided, then the different nations would unite to eradicate the problems of AIDS and other diseases, the growing gap between rich and poor, and pollution and other environmental problems. But humanity isn't united, so ending our religious and political divisions should be our greatest priority.

The first problem in the survey: the spread of nuclear weapons, worries some countries more than others. However, the root cause of nuclear proliferation is the same throughout the world: it's that people are religiously and politically divided. This was true when nuclear proliferation began during the Cold War because it pitted the Christian and capitalist USA against the socialist and atheist USSR. It's still true today because of the religious and political differences between India and Pakistan, and between Israel and its neighbors. Moreover, as long as North Korea is separated from the rest of the world, their nuclear weapons will also remain a threat.

The cure for nuclear proliferation isn't a treaty, especially when Israel, India, and Pakistan are non-signatories to the Nuclear Non-Proliferation Treaty, when North Korea withdrew its signature, and when there are concerns that Iran will violate this treaty. The Nuclear Non-Proliferation Treaty also won't stop terrorists or rogue states from seeking and using nuclear weapons. The only way to ensure that nuclear, chemical, biological, and conventional weapons won't get used is to get everyone religiously and politically united.

Of course, it might seem unlikely that our world will ever be religiously and politically united. However, the natural course of history is for people to slowly adopt similar beliefs. This is most obvious where science has united people around similar beliefs. Although not as obvious, the world's religious and political organizations have also become more alike as they have also been forced to embrace more advanced beliefs.

As women and minorities gain equal rights and as the opposition towards birth control, same-sex marriage, and the teaching of evolution dissipates, the major religions and the major political parties have had no choice but to accept modern and, thus, similar beliefs about women, minorities, birth control, evolution, and human sexuality. This transformation isn't happening quickly and it isn't occurring without opposition, but it's happening fast enough to alter the religious and political environment for each successive generation.

Religious and political progress can be difficult to see because it usually occurs slowly. Yet we only need to look back a short distance in time to see how steady religious and political progress has been. For example, going back just 100 years in time and women couldn't vote or attain high positions in most of the major religions or corporations. Back then, most minorities were also denied upper-level jobs and civil and political rights. Furthermore, birth control, the teaching of evolution, and interracial, interfaith, and same-sex marriages were also unlawful or against most religious doctrines. Fast forward to the present and most women can vote, human rights are far more widespread, and evolution, birth control, interracial, interfaith, and same-sex relations are accepted in most modern countries.

Clearly, religious and political progress doesn't happen fast enough for most of us. But it is constantly occurring.

One reason change is so slow is those who have the most power (the older generations) are the most conservative members of society. Although polls verify that the older generations are more conservative than the younger generations, there hasn't been enough polling to verify the old cliché that people switch from liberal to conservative as they age.

What Gallup and the Pew Research Center found in 2017 is that although society is more partisan than ever before, society is shifting to the left and, not surprisingly, this leftward shift is most pronounced among young people. So even though many conservatives disparage the term "liberal," society is continually becoming more liberal.

According to Pew in 2016, "as in recent years, Millennials and Gen Xers were the most Democratic generations. And both groups had relatively large – and growing – shares of liberal Democrats." Pew also found that young republicans were more moderate and liberal than older republicans. Yet even though our religious and political evolution is steady and inevitable, many people resist and even deny it. Perhaps this is because stable, unwavering beliefs seem like an accomplishment. But stable, unwavering beliefs are absurd because we don't fully understand ourselves, the universe, and God.

Another sign that society is becoming more liberal is the recent decrease in traditional religions and the rapid increase in the other side of the spectrum: people who say they have no religious affiliation. The rise in the unaffiliated is a shift to the left because the vast majority of the unaffiliated (73%) vote Democratic and are politically liberal.

Could a decrease in religious affiliation bring us together and reduce the threat of nuclear war? It should because it's part of a larger trend that includes greater religious tolerance and more interfaith marriages. Added together, these are all signs that the world's religions are losing their ability to define and divide people.

With each passing year, there are less people who define themselves with a religious label and more people who see themselves as just human beings. If this trend continues, then the nuclear powers separated by religious identity, such as: Israel, India, and Pakistan will also lose their ability to define and divide people. More importantly, if this trend continues, there won't be enough adherents to support the major religions and, in a few decades, all that will be left to divide people will be race, nationality, political ideology, and social class.

Luckily, there aren't any nuclear tensions between the different races, social classes, or political parties, so nationalism is the only other threat for nuclear war. Yet the rivalry between different nations is also disappearing as governments throughout the world strengthen trade relationships.

Like the advancements in the world's religions, political progress also isn't swift, obvious, or without opposition. Yet, once again, we only need look back about 100 years to see how much the world's political landscape has advanced and unified.

A century ago, most nations in Europe, the Americas, and Asia were continually at war and there was also internal strife within most nations over whether communism, or capitalism was best. Today, most nations in Europe, Asia, and the Americas have peaceful relations and most nations have also adopted a combination of capitalism with social programs.

Even though political unity also seems unlikely when we look at the present state of the world, political progress is continually occurring. This is because literacy, education, and modern culture are continually spreading, which continually pushes our religious and political beliefs forward.

As people become more educated, they adopt similar and more liberal political beliefs. According to Pew in 2016, "registered voters with a college degree or more education favor Clinton over Trump by 23 percentage points (52% Clinton vs. 29% Trump). By contrast, voters who do not have a college degree were more divided in their preferences: 41% backed Trump, 36% Clinton, 9% Johnson and 5% Stein." This also shows that the solution to the first problem in the survey: nuclear proliferation, is education which encourages the natural and ongoing evolution in our religious and political thought because it's slowly, yet persistently creates a more liberal and unified world.

The second problem in the survey: religious and ethnic hatred, is easier to tie to our religious and political divisions because it should be obvious how these divisions pit one group of people against another. But here too there is hope for the future because polls consistently show that the younger generations are more tolerant about religious and ethnic differences than the older generations.

According to a 2010 report by the Pew Research Center,

> Generations, like people, have personalities, and Millennials--the American teens and twenty-somethings who were making the passage into adulthood at the start of a new millennium--have begun to forge theirs: confident, self-expressive, liberal, upbeat and open to change.
>
> They are more ethnically and racially diverse than older adults. They're less religious, less likely to have served in the military, and are on track to become the most educated generation in American history.

The older a person is, the more emphasis they place on their racial and religious identity. But the future is created by the youth, who polls show are increasingly colorblind and "spiritual but not religious."

It was the young people throughout North Africa and the Middle East, now called the Internet or Facebook generation, who mobilized in opposition to the oppressive regimes, calling for democracy, women's rights, and economic reforms in countries once controlled by military and religious dictators. Although many people hoped that the Arab Spring would immediately bring freedom to the Middle East, change is rarely quick or painless. Another problem is that many of the wars in the Middle East are intensified by overpopulation and global warming, and these threats will also take decades to resolve.

The challenge of bringing North Korea into the modern world is that the internet and other foreign print and broadcast media are unavailable to the average North Korean. This keeps the people in North Korea from progressing along with the rest of the world. Luckily, many North Koreans have been smuggling in cell phones, computers, and foreign movies, so they might be more aware of the modern world than we and their own government realize.

The last three problems in the survey: AIDS and other infectious diseases, pollution and other environmental problems, and the growing gap between rich and poor may not be caused by our religious and political differences, but they have the same cure: that we work together to solve them. Unfortunately, many powerful religious and political lobbies throughout the world still demonize homosexuality and the use of contraceptives, which doesn't help slow the spread of AIDS. Furthermore, many religious and political leaders don't agree that pollution, infectious diseases, and the growing gap between rich and poor are serious problems, which is why they haven't received the attention needed to reduce their growth. But, as always, there is hope for the future because polls consistently show that each generation is more accepting of homosexuality and the use of contraceptives than the previous generation. Also, the two problems in the survey to show the greatest increase in concern throughout the world were pollution and the growing gap between rich and poor, so these problems should also get more attention as time goes by.

Even overpopulation, which wasn't listed as a threat in the survey, but which many people feel multiplies all our other problems could be reduced if we were united to ensuring women's rights and universal access to family planning. But our ability to guarantee women's rights and access to family planning is also limited by our religious and political divisions, so, once again, a serious problem has the same cure: that we encourage progress in our religious and political beliefs. Unfortunately, that's easier said than done because everyone is supposed to know that it's impolite to discuss religion and politics.

Haven't we all been told as children not to discuss religion and politics with strangers? And who hasn't been warned as an adult not to discuss religion and politics at the dinner table, even if we are with friends and family? So maybe this is our greatest problem: we can't easily discuss the two subjects that divide us.

The greatest challenge facing humanity isn't nuclear war, overpopulation, or global warming; it's that few people are willing to discuss their religious and political beliefs. This isn't to say that people aren't willing to push their religious and political beliefs in person or online, but that there is an unwillingness to objectively discuss and, more importantly, alter one's beliefs. It's this lack of openness and objectivity that divides us, slows religious and political progress, and ultimately keeps us from eliminating war, environmental degradation, overpopulation, government corruption, and disease.

Chapter Five

Obstacles

Understanding why it's so difficult to examine our beliefs is our most urgent challenge. And it's a substantial challenge because our beliefs don't have a taste, smell, sound, feel, or visual appearance that science can measure.

What cognitive scientists like Joshua Greene and Fiery Cushman have discovered by studying how different areas of the brain are activated by moral and philosophical questioning is that people rely more on emotions than logic to make decisions. They also found that emotional decisions are faster and take less energy than logic. This led them to conclude that the emotional and cognitive parts of the brain are at odds and engage in a sort of "neural tug-of-war" between emotional responses that are fast and easy and cognitive responses that are slow and energy consuming.

In a 2016 interview with Lauren Cassani Davis in the Atlantic Magazine,

> You describe moral decision-making as a process that combines two types of thinking: "manual" thinking that is slow, consciously controlled, and rule-based, and "automatic" mental processes that are fast, emotional, and effortless. How widespread is this "dual-process" theory of the human mind?
>
> Joshua Greene, "I haven't encountered any evidence that has caused me to rethink the basic idea that automatic and controlled processing make distinct contributions to judgment and decision making. Thanks primarily to Daniel Kahneman [the author of Thinking, Fast and Slow] and

Amos Tversky, and everything that follows them, it's the dominant perspective in judgment and decision making."

For most of human history, we needed quick, emotional reactions to dangerous animals, stinging insects, and enemy combatants as much as we needed to slowly and logically plan for food storage, home building, and tool making. But in the modern world, our need for quick, emotional reactions has almost disappeared while our need to make slow, complex decisions at work and home has substantially increased.

The modern world requires less impulse and more contemplation about things that our ancestors didn't need to worry about, such as: obesity, overpopulation, and global warming. To avoid these dangers, we don't need to react quickly, we need to slow down and think more deeply.

A paper published in 2010 by Matthew Feinberg and Robb Willer of the University of California, Berkeley reveals another reason why life's complex and challenging nature actually drives people away from rational beliefs and behaviors. Their paper focused on the belief in global warming and how "dire messages reduce belief in global warming even though scientific evidence for the existence of global warming continues to mount."

Their paper states:

> "research shows that many individuals have a strong need to perceive the world as just – believing that future rewards await those who judiciously strive for them, and punishments are meted out to those who deserve them (Dalbert, 2001; Furnham, 2003). Research on Just World Theory has demonstrated that when an individual's need to believe in a just world is threatened, they commonly employ defensive responses, such as dismissing or rationalizing the information that threatened their just world beliefs (for reviews, see Furnham, 2003; Hafer & Bégue, 2005). Information regarding the potentially severe and arbitrary effects of global warming should constitute a significant threat to a belief in a just world, and discrediting

or denying global warming's existence could serve as a means of resolving the resulting threat."

It should come as no surprise that many people want to believe in a positive future, especially for those who have been good. Yet there is evidence that global warming won't create a positive future, especially for the younger generations who have done the least to create global warming. This unfairness upsets many people and causes them to embrace simpler stories that compete with the evidence.

Of course, other people deny man-made global warming because of their desire to profit from the coal and oil industry. Perhaps most troubling is a 2017 study by Matto Mildenberger and Anthony Leiserowitz from the Yale Program on Climate Change Communication, which shows that, "Public opinion on climate change is very sensitive to changes in the Republican and Democratic party platforms and politicians' talking points,"

It seems that our recent decent into partisan politics is also driving the debate on climate change. It appears that many conservatives would rather stay in their political party than consider the evidence.

Politicians are also worried that following their conscience and accepting the evidence on man-made global warming could make them a target in the primaries. As Nadja Popovich, John Schwartz and Tatiana Schlossberg wrote in the New York Times on 3-21-2017.

> Bob Inglis, a former Republican congressman from South Carolina, warned that committed activists — like the Tea Party — can shape politicians' approaches to issues like climate change. "Those are the ones who can take you out at the next primary," he said. Mr. Inglis lost his primary in 2010 to Trey Gowdy, a Tea Party candidate who attacked his climate views.

Current resistance to the scientific consensus on global warming comes mainly from republican groups funded by the fossil fuel industry. Yet denying the facts because they're economically inconvenient to the funders of your group is also irrational when climate change is the most significant threat facing our world.

Studies have shown that there are two major barriers to being a rational person. The first is that rational thought takes time and energy and causes stress, and we are instinctively driven to conserve energy, avoid stress, and react quickly. The second barrier is that even if a person takes the time, expends the energy, and endures the stress to understand the facts, the facts may not depict the reality that they or their group wants to see, and this creates an emotional dislike and conscious fear of rational thought.

Ignorance isn't caused just by poverty, mismanaged schools, or even a lack of facts. Ignorance is also caused by our innate dislike of stress and exertion and our conscious and emotional fear of learning about our complex and challenging world. Unfortunately, these internal drivers of ignorance are more challenging to eradicate than the external forces of poverty and bad schools because human nature can't be altered with a government policy.

We won't understand humanity and our self-destructiveness unless we acknowledge how challenging reality is to learn about and accept. Perhaps to understand the true scope of self-inflicted ignorance, we need to examine a few basic frustrations with reality.

It isn't just larger issues like evolution and global warming that cause people to turn away from learning; it's also smaller, everyday issues, like learning about all the pleasures we must avoid to maintain our health that cause people to turn away from the pursuit of knowledge. It's that everyone finds it physically strenuous and emotionally upsetting to learn about all the foods, behaviors, and intoxicants we must avoid to remain healthy.

Every child is frustrated to learn that they can't stay up as late as they want and that they can't eat all the candy they want. This is where the frustration with reality begins: in our youth.

Humans don't fall from the sky as fully formed adults who are completely open to different ideas and behaviors. We are born as completely ignorant children who are instinctively driven to find pleasure and avoid pain. Moreover, our youthful ignorance causes us to believe that we can attain all the pleasures we desire and avoid all the pains we dislike. Unfortunately, we quickly learn that our parents won't let us have everything we want. This frustration is compounded when we learn that it wasn't simply our parents' cruelty that kept us from having and doing everything we want; it was and is the laws of reality that prevent us from having and doing everything we want.

Growing up is a process of learning that reality is not Utopia. It's a process of learning that reality does not allow us to easily or completely fulfill all of our desires. Life then becomes a process of deciding whether we are willing to face reality and restrict our diet, drug use, and sexual behaviors so we can remain healthy, or whether we're going to do what's most pleasurable at the moment even if it's ultimately self-destructive.

Unfortunately, more people do what's most pleasurable at the moment than what's healthiest over the long term. This impulsiveness is largely due to the fact that humans evolved in a harsh wilderness where life was short and strenuous and offered few options. Fortunately, life is no longer so short and difficult. But our impulses now work against us because the modern world offers so many sedentary jobs and such easy access to drugs, junk food, and random sex partners. In the modern world, impulse control is what's needed.

Although people like to say that, "The truth will set you free," in reality, the truth will restrict your behavior, or it will make you realize that you should control your impulses. That's why we have a competing saying, "Ignorance is bliss."

The more we learn about nutrition, the less free we become because the more we learn how we should restrict our diet. Similarly, the more we learn about sexually transmitted diseases, the less free we become because the more we learn how dangerous some sexual behaviors are. In that sense, knowledge sets us free by revealing the healthiest path. But the healthiest path is rarely the freest, easiest, or most pleasurable path, especially over the short term.

Evolution and global warming are not the only issues that people have with reality because they are not the only difficult and frustrating concepts that we must learn about. Instead, most of reality is difficult and frustrating to learn about. And if we don't acknowledge all the smaller challenges that life throws at us from childhood, then we won't understand why so many adults lack the ability to discuss larger issues like evolution and global warming.

It may seem like only religious fanatics are ignoring science and only because certain scientific theories conflict with scripture. Yet everyone has grievances with science and the reality it uncovers. For example, who wasn't upset by the recent scientific discovery that the carbs we crave, like cookies and french-fries are unhealthy, while the vegetables we don't crave, like broccoli and cabbage are the foods we should eat every day?

How many people are truly happy to learn about nutrition, or about the fact that the sweetest and most pleasurable foods are almost always the least healthy foods? Not me and probably not you, so although it's easy to scorn religious fanatics for ignoring science, it's difficult to admit that we too wish some scientific facts weren't true.

We won't understand ourselves and humanity's self-destructiveness if we think that only some people have issues with reality. To understand our global inability to chart a healthier course, we need to understand why everyone has some desire to turn away from reality.

As always, the best historical example of how our innate desire to ignore reality has shaped society comes from Galileo. And the first barrier to accepting Galileo's discoveries was the mental effort required to understand that, although it seems like everything is revolving around the Earth, in reality, we live in a sun centered solar system. The second barrier to accepting Galileo's discoveries was the emotional fortitude needed to admit that we aren't the center of the universe. Finally, just like going against one's religious or political group today, it also took mental effort and emotional strength to go against the Catholic Church and all the power it wielded.

It's impossible to know how many people didn't accept Galileo's discoveries because they were too mentally lazy to consider his more complicated picture of our solar system, how many didn't accept Galileo's discoveries because they were too emotionally frail to admit that the universe doesn't revolve around them, and how many just didn't want to go against the dominant social, religious, and political group. All we can know for sure is Galileo's ideas took more effort to learn about and courage to accept than many of his contemporaries were willing to impart.

Chapter Six

Groups

Life is so challenging to learn about that a majority of people may never have rational beliefs. Instead, humanity may always be divided into different groups because only a minority of people may put forth the effort to be rational, while another fraction may always seek a simpler and more pleasing picture of our world, while still another group may always have no interest in and no opinions about the topics that require rational thought.

A 2009 Gallup poll taken on the 200th anniversary of Darwin's birthday revealed how society is divided into these 3 groups: the rational, the zealous, and the indifferent. This poll found that 39% of people believe in evolution, 25% do not believe in evolution, and 36% have no opinion either way. When the respondent's level of education and church attendance was factored in, it became clear why society is divided into these three groups.

The more often a respondent went to church, the more likely they were to say that they didn't believe in evolution, going up to 41% for those who attend church weekly compared to only 25% for the general population. No surprise here because we're all familiar with the battle between science and religion. What's surprising is that the less educated respondents didn't have much of an increase in the disbelief in evolution, increasing only 2% for those with a high school education or less. What distinguishes the uneducated is how much more likely they were to say that they have no opinion about evolution, jumping up to 52% compared to 36% for the general population.

This poll reveals two correlations. The first and most familiar correlation is between higher religious zeal and a higher disbelief in scientific facts. The second and less talked about correlation is between lower education levels and lower opinion levels.

This poll doesn't prove that religiosity and a disbelief in evolution spring from an emotional dissatisfaction with reality, nor does it prove that not pursing higher education and having no opinions spring from a dislike of or inability to engage in extended mental exertion. Yet, as mentioned earlier, neuroscientists have evidence that humans naturally resist difficult mental deliberations and psychologists have evidence that people resist factual beliefs when those beliefs are emotionally displeasing, so this poll lends support to the idea that people are choosing their beliefs based on the physical and emotional challenges posed by different beliefs.

In the not too distant future, scientists may quantify how much effort is required to learn about different concepts. This should be possible because brain scans already reveal *where* in our brain there is increased blood flow because of the increase in oxygen and glucose metabolism needed for different mental activities, so all scientists would have to do is measure *how many calories* are spent because of this increased blood flow and oxygen and glucose metabolism.

Perhaps scientists will figure out how many calories and, thus, how much effort is required to become proficient in subjects like biology and astronomy. This effort, or this caloric expenditure required for learning should help explain why so many people resist complex ideas. Of course, the physical effort needed to read and study is only half the prerequisite for learning. The other prerequisite is the emotional ability to go against one's group and accept that Planet Earth isn't so simple.

Scientists may be able to figure out how many calories it takes to learn about subjects like biology and astronomy, but scientists may not be able to fully explain why people have different beliefs about biology and astronomy because it may not be possible to quantify the *emotional barriers* that stands in the way of accepting such emotionally charged ideas as: "we are related to the lower animals" and "we are not the center of the universe." Scientists may only be able to explain the physical barriers to learning because physical barriers are overcome through the tangible process of "exertion," while emotional challenges are overcome through the intangible process of "maturity."

Theoretically, there should be a quantifiable caloric requirement to learning all the facts of evolution, but there probably isn't a quantifiable emotional expense to accepting the idea that we are related to the lower animals. There may also not be a quantifiable emotional expense to accepting that your religious group is wrong about evolution. This is why we may never have a scientific explanation of our beliefs and behaviors: humans are not purely physical beings who are affected only by physical forces.

Although the human body is a machine, our brain reacts to what no other machine reacts to: ideas. Or we react to the meaning of an idea, whereas all other machines react only to the physical strain of absorbing the bites of information contained in different ideas.

Computers don't feel rejection, defeat, disgust, jealousy, sadness, fear, self-pity, and so on when downloading an emotionally charged idea. This is why humans are so much more complex than computers: we often have an emotional response to the information entering our processor and memory.

Because our reaction to the "meaning" of an idea can't be explained physically, our beliefs and behaviors can't be explained scientifically. The problem is science can't explain how the meaning of an idea could upset some people, inspire other people, and cause still other people to shut down their thought process altogether.

The primary challenge of explaining human nature is that we are conscious being who possess free will, or we seem to be conscious beings who possess free will. Again, this is why every discussion of human behavior falls into the realm of philosophy: scientists can't verify if we have free will.

Scientists can't verify if we are consciously choosing our beliefs and behaviors, or if everything we do and believe is determined by past events and the laws of physics. This means that before we can identify the causes behind our beliefs and behaviors, we must take a stand on free will. Again, my position is if we lack free will and are unable to choose our beliefs and behaviors, then life is meaningless and there is nothing to discuss. To put it another way, the only reason to discuss the physical, mental, and emotional obstacles to becoming a rational person is because we believe that people can choose to overcome those barriers.

All advice is worthless if we lack free will. This is why it's difficult to deny free will: it requires believing that you, your children, and everyone else is unable to control themselves. Obviously, it's ludicrous to believe that we all lack self-control. But if we believe in free will, then another dilemma arises: we must accept that science can't explain all the motivations behind our beliefs and behaviors.

If you believe in free will, then you must not expect science to completely explain our beliefs and behaviors. Instead, you must accept that a mixture of science and logic is needed to explain humanity.

If humans possess free will, then we must use science and logic to explain why 24% of the respondents in the above Gallup poll who attended church weekly were still able to accept evolution. We must also use science and logic to explain why 26% of the respondents who graduated from college and 16% of the respondents who earned postgraduate degrees still had no opinions about evolution. We must use science and logic to explain how religious people can believe in evolution and how people can spend years in college and end up with no opinions.

The primary obstacle to getting evolution more widely accepted may seem to come from creationists. Yet the above Gallup poll revealed that there are 11% more people who have no opinion about evolution than there are people who disbelieve evolution. If humans lack free will, then these differing beliefs about evolution are due to long chains of chemical reactions that stretch all the way back to the big bang. But who cares if life is just an unalterable chemical reaction? What we should care about is that if people possess free will, then apathy is shaping society more than is the desire to have an emotional pleasing belief.

It's sad that most arguments about evolution are between scientists and religious individuals because religious people make up a smaller percentage of the population who don't embrace evolution. Of course, scientists end up arguing with religious people because it's impossible to argue with people who have no opinions. However, if we are truly concerned about scientific literacy, then we shouldn't ignore the fact that 11% more people have no opinion about evolution than actually disbelieve evolution.

Perhaps more people have no opinion about evolution than actually disbelieve evolution because it's easier to have no opinion than to embrace even the simplest of religion. This makes sense because if people possess free will, then logic indicates that people would use their free will to take the thought process of least resistance.

Luckily, the youngest adults, those between 18-34 years-old, contains the most people who believe in evolution--49%, the least who do not believe in evolution--18%, and the least who have no opinion either way--33%. This shows that logic propagates through time and that being young and energetic makes logic and learning easier. It shows that society should continue to advance as time goes by.

Unfortunately, 33% of young adults having no opinion about evolution shows that a large chunk of society may always be indifferent and oblivious to science. It shows that reality may always be too physically, mentally, and/or emotionally demanding for large numbers of people.

Chapter Seven

Logic

In the fall of 2010, a few hundred-people attended a conference near the campus of the University of Notre Dame entitled, "Galileo Was Wrong." This was an embarrassment to what many people feel is America's flagship Catholic University. Yet supporters contend that there is scientific evidence for an Earth centered solar system just as they say there is evidence for the six-day story of creation in the book of Genesis.

Perhaps some people feel that they can defend the bible against the ideas of Galileo and Darwin because these discoveries were based on observations that could be flawed. But how does one defend the bible against its acceptance of slavery when our own logic refutes this teaching?

Most Christians now repudiate slavery even though the Bible is filled with passages that endorse slavery and even though many Christian leaders throughout history, like Jefferson Davis, the first and only President of the Confederate States of America often used the Bible to defend slavery. Here is Jefferson Davis's most popular quote using the bible to defend slavery:

> "It [slavery] was established by decree of Almighty God...it is sanctioned in the Bible, in both Testaments, from Genesis to Revelation...Slavery existed then in the earliest ages, and among the chosen people of God; and in Revelation we are told that it shall exist till the end of time shall come. In the prophecies, psalms, and the epistles of Paul; you find it recognized, sanctioned everywhere."

If the Bible endorses slavery everywhere, then why do most Christians now refute slavery? Why did even the Southern Baptists, the staunchest supporters of slavery, formally renounce the church's support of slavery and segregation in 1995? Obviously, people can use logic to nullify the claims of religion. But if history shows that people can and have used logic to invalidate biblical teachings, why do people persist in claiming that religion is unchangeable and above human logic? The question is, "How much is religious fanaticism driven by a physical dislike of exerting our brain, how much is driven by an emotional dislike of difficult and complex ideas, and how much is driven by a desire to control or be part of a group?"

The most prominent religious figure to recently claim that religion is unchangeable by human logic was Pope John Paul II. In 1994, he declared that, "The Church does not have the power to ordain women." He formally stated:

> "Although the teaching that priestly ordination is to be reserved to men alone has been preserved by the constant and universal tradition of the Church and firmly taught by the magisterium in its more recent documents, at the present time in some places it is nonetheless considered still open to debate, or the Church's judgment that women are not to be admitted to ordination is considered to have a merely disciplinary force. Wherefore, in order that all doubt may be removed regarding a matter of great importance, a matter which pertains to the Church's divine constitution itself, in virtue of my ministry of confirming the brethren (cf. Luke 22:32) I declare that the Church has no authority whatsoever to confer priestly ordination on women and that this judgment is to be definitively held by all the Church's faithful" (*Ordinatio Sacerdotalis* 4).

Now that the Catholic Church has apologized to Galileo, teaches evolution in its schools, and rejects slavery, how many people really believe that the Catholic Church has "no power" and "no authority" to go further and ordain women? After all the other changes made by the Catholic Church, how many people would make any serious wager that the Catholic Church won't change again and accept women as being completely equal to men?

Strangely, although Pope Francis softened the Catholic Church's stand on homosexuality during an interview in the summer of 2013, he went on to state that the ordained ministry would never include women because Pope John Paul II expressly forbade it. But why do women always gain their rights after all other groups? Why did the 15th amendment, which prohibited denying a citizen the right to vote based on race, color, and previous servitude say nothing about denying a citizen the right to vote based on gender? Why did women's suffrage take another 50 years?

Although most religions and many governments claim to be divinely inspired, it seems a bit terrestrial that most religions and many governments place men above women. Rather than being God's desire, it's far more logical that patriarchy is the standard religious and government policy because the instinctive desire of most male animals is to have power over the females.

It's a bit more difficult to figure out why women would attend church more frequently than men when most religions are patriarchal. Perhaps this is also instinctive. Perhaps because of the long-term hardships of pregnancy and child-rearing, women have always needed and, thus, have always instinctively wanted men to take care of them. Perhaps this instinctive desire to be sheltered by men is why the "Catholic Answers' website" would post and expect women in the 21st century to accept the following scriptures:

> "While women could publicly pray and prophesy in church (1 Cor. 11:1–16), they could not teach or have authority over a man (1 Tim. 2:11–14), since these were two essential functions of the clergy. Nor could women publicly question or challenge the teaching of the clergy (1 Cor. 14:34–38)."

Most religions continue to place men above women and most religions have endorsed slavery or the caste system for fairly simple and for clearly earthly reasons: these relationships satisfy basic human desires. Again, I'm not going to argue scripture because it's difficult to believe that God wants slavery, patriarchy, or the caste system. It makes far more sense that human nature lies at the root of these traditions. This is also why it's so difficult to rid our world of outdated religious traditions: it's difficult to abandon behaviors that are favored by evolution and driven by instinct.

Although the world's religions speak to our conscience by teaching compassion, humility, and sacrifice, there is another side to religion. This side speaks to our instinctive urges and it often negates the positive side of religion.

Religion would be easier to embrace or abandon if it was monolithic. But religion, like everything else we humans do is a battle. It's a battle because we have higher and lower desires, or we have desires that come from our conscience and desires that come from our instincts.

The pioneering psychologist William James, proposed that humans were motivated by instincts back in the 1880s. Of course, this wasn't desirable to hear back then because instinct was associated with animals. Another problem with claiming that humans possess instinct is that many modern scientists want instinct to be defined as something that can't be overridden. Yet we can override most of our drives, even our drives for sex and food.

Although humans can override their most basic desires, humans are not born as blank slates. Because we don't learn all our behaviors, humans can be said to possess instinct. For example, we don't learn to prefer sweet over sour, easy over difficult, or warm over cold. These preferences are all innate, or instinctive.

The denial of human instinct is harmful for three main reasons. First, it keeps us ignorant of the true source of our motivation. Second, it allows people to blame straw-men like the devil for our behavior. Third, it implies that all behaviors are consciously chosen, which leads to the naïve belief that people can easily choose new behaviors and that all we have to do to change a person's undesirable habits is tell them about healthier behaviors.

If our bad habits were truly caused by the devil, then dieticians, personal trainers, and addition specialists would only need to learn how to protect people from the devil. On the other hand, if all unhealthy behaviors were simply uniformed choices, then dieticians, personal trainers, and addition specialists would only need to hand out a list of better choices. But being healthy isn't as easy as getting an exorcism or a fitness book. Instead, being healthy is a lifelong struggle for everyone because we must all continually fight against our body's innate desires and impulses.

In the last century, the denial of human instinct led to the belief that males and females behave differently only because of culture, which led to the rather harmless attempt to raise boys and girls in gender neutral environments. More damaging was the attempt to actually turn boys into girls and vice versa by forcing young children to adopt opposing sexual roles. One of the most well publicized cases was the attempt to raise David Reimer, a healthy boy as girl because of a botched circumcision he received in 1966 at the age of 8 months. At 22 months, David was given sexual reassignment surgery and the name Brenda. Although his sexual reassignment was hailed as a success for many years, it actually made "Brenda" unhappy enough to contemplate suicide at age 13. By age 14, Brenda began living as a boy again and when he was 31, David went public to discourage sexual reassignment on children who are too young to consent. Along with other studies of how boys and girls freely choose different toys and play activities, the failed sexual reassignment of David Reimer makes it clear that humans are born with innate desires and that culture can only slightly suppress our innate preferences.

Most scientists now accept that the slate we are working on isn't blank but is scrawled all over with instinct. Yet many people still want to believe that human behavior is one-dimensional and purely the product of our mind and culture because it's far more challenging and far less flattering to accept that we are also motivated by instinct.

Of course, it's even more difficult and less flattering to accept that our religions and cultures are also more a product of our instincts than a product of our mind. This led Matt Ridley to explain how culture is often just the result of nature in his 2003 book Nature via Nurture, "There might be all sorts of cultural aspects to a behavior that is grounded in instinct. Culture will often reflect human nature rather than affect it."

It's flattering to hear that our beliefs and behaviors are motivated by honest and extended contemplations and that our cultures and religions are also shaped by these noble and extensive deliberations. But the cultural and religious opposition to the well-thought-out ideas of Galileo, Darwin, and the anti-slavery movement make it clear that our cultures and religions are inspired more by our short-sighted impulses, fears, and desires than by our conscience. What should be clear is that our instincts shape our religions as much, if not more than our religions subdue our instincts. Most importantly, our religions can't help us subdue our instincts as long as they deny our evolution from the lower animals.

Our conscience does affect us and many great minds have shaped our religions and societies. But our instincts affect us first. Moreover, instinct has guided our ancestors' behavior for millions of years, while religion and the language needed to convey complex religious ideas have been advanced enough to offer a real alternative to our innate impulses for only a few thousand years.

Culture is defined as the passing on of skills, knowledge, and behaviors. This goes back to the beginning of our species, and some will argue that culture exists in other species. But what's important is that culture did not arise one day and eliminate our instincts the next day. Instead, culture slowly added skills, motivations, and inhibitions to the instinctive skills, motivations, and inhibitions we are born with.

Some people say that empathy and compassion come from religion and/or culture. But empathy and compassion arose as soon as our ape-ancestors formed social groups because their real strength was not in their teeth or claws, but in their ability to cooperate.

Of course, other people argue that war and aggression come from religion and/or culture. But war and aggression also arose long before religion appeared because our ancestors always needed to be capable of aggression so they could defend their mates and territory.

Although many people blame religion for all the good and bad in our world, religion has not been around long enough to deserve all the blame. Religion is more of a recent excuse than a root cause.

Even when our hunter/gatherer ancestors started to evolve into farmers and herders about 10 thousand years ago, they still needed to defend themselves against those who would steal their land, mates, and livestock. So even though our ancestors were continually evolving more social natures, they always needed to have somewhat aggressive natures or they would be overrun by more aggressive people.

Competition for scarce resources is one of the oldest and most fundamental drivers of evolution. But many people want to blame this newcomer called religion for all the conflicts between people. Yet war didn't arise with religion; religion just offered a justification for why our tribe should prevail in the ongoing territorial battles to control the resources.

As hunter/gatherers evolved into farmers and herders and finally into urban dwellers, our cultures were governed less by the shortsighted brutality of instinct and more by logic, reason, and compassion. This is confirmed by Lawrence H. Keeley, a professor of archaeology at the University of Illinois at Chicago who has shown how death from war and murder is more common the farther back in time we travel. However, our increasing civility may not be caused solely by our evolving more peaceful natures and cultures. It may be caused by our evolving technologies that allow us to produce more food so there isn't so much competition for resources. This is verified by the recent increase in wars and genocides in Africa and the Middle East where our agricultural technologies have failed to keep pace with the increase in population and the depletion of groundwater.

It's easy to believe in the absolute that humans evolved to be either aggressive, or compassionate. Yet the more complicated truth is we evolved to be aggressive to those who threaten us and compassionate to those who help us. Even more confounding is that each person has a different amount of aggression and compassion in their personality.

There isn't one type of person in our world. Instead, there are highly compassionate people and there are psychopaths, sociopaths, and narcissists in our world. These variations may exist because psychopaths, sociopaths, and narcissists survive better in times of war and scarcity, while compassionate people produce healthier offspring when there are sufficient resources.

Humans have diverse personalities because we evolved in diverse and constantly changing environments. Yet if you believe that humans didn't evolve but were created in their present form by God about 6,000 years ago, then all the variations between people are difficult to understand.

Conflicts between people are difficult to eliminate because humans evolved to compete with other humans and other species. Similarly, it's difficult to unify the different races, religions, and political groups because we evolved in small tribal groups where we had to fear people we didn't recognize. Certainly, we can learn to be more compassionate, and our religions should help us to become more compassionate, but our natural impulse is to compete with and be wary of others, which is why so many religions are so tribalistic.

Religion isn't the primary or the only motivator of behavior and, thus, it isn't the only or the primary creator of culture. Behavior is and culture was shaped first by our lower impulses.

Culture isn't created only by those who are interested in religious and philosophical enlightenment. Culture is also created by those who are angry, greedy, cowardly, apathetic, impulsive, self-destructive, and ignorant of the larger problems that face our world. Culture is a battle, or it's a democratic process, which is why so many people dislike the outcome.

Culture isn't the result of a one day, society-wide, intellectual battle between two opposing philosophies where the winner takes all. Culture is the result of millions of individuals all struggling with their own conscience and impulses. Unfortunately, these individual-struggles often produce racist, sexist, and xenophobic subcultures that are distasteful, which is why so many people try to ignore these individual struggles and pretend that culture is created only by the cultured.

Human behavior can be loathsome and this causes many people to turn away from honest discussions of human behavior. It causes many people to see no evil, hear no evil, and insist that all behaviors are motivated by the conscience, which they can easily influence with a debate.

Although many people are motivated by their conscience, many others don't care about our debates and many don't deserve credit for having a religion because all that many people have are shortsighted and self-centered motivations. Yet our dislike of unpleasant conversations causes many people to ignore the instinctive side of human behavior and trust completely in what people state is their motivation.

Believing that religion is the sole motivation for war, child marriage, gender bias, and homophobia is to believe that our instincts don't exist. It's to ignore our primary motivations which just increases the ignorance of human behavior, and that only makes it easier for the frauds and swindlers to get away with even more criminal behavior. It's to ignore the fact that in Gallup's 45 years of polling, women score significantly higher than men in five categories: the importance of religion in their lives, church/synagogue membership and attendance, the belief that religion can answer most of today's problems, the role of God in their personal decision-making, and weekly Bible reading and group Bible study, but men are more responsible for war, child marriage, gender bias, and homophobia than women. Obviously, if religion was the cause of war, child marriage, gender bias, and homophobia, then women would be more responsible for these problems than they are.

Chapter Eight

Ideology

In 2010, researchers at the University of Toronto found that the concern for compassion and equality is associated with a liberal mindset, while the concern for order and respect of social norms is associated with a conservative mindset. Research has also shown that people usually vote according to their personality, or for the left if their personality allows for more experimentation and for the right if their personality makes them more cautious.

It shouldn't be surprising that some people have a liberal personality, while others have a conservative personality. It also shouldn't be surprising that people tend to flock together with those who have a personality like theirs. What should be troubling is that our desire to be part of a like-minded group is corrupting our logic and ethics because this tribalism is causing people to care more about a politician's personality and group affiliation than about their honesty and integrity.

It would be best if political races were determined solely by policy discussions, but numerous studies show, and Donald Trump's defeat of "boring" Jeb Bush show that a politician's personality is really what attracts the votes. Similarly, it would be best if our religions were shaped solely by theological discussions, but years of research into what makes churches successful shows that churchgoers care more about the preacher's personality than about his or her theology.

Research has shown that religion and politics are shaped more by our emotions than our intellect. Therefore, the most important step to religious and political progress is to increase everyone's understanding of human nature so everyone will understand how emotions and impulses usually underlie what are portrayed to be intellectually grounded political ideologies and divinely inspired scriptures.

With all the emotions and cults of personality infusing religion and politics it might seem like only the objective methods of science could advance religion and politics. Yet science hasn't solved our religious and political arguments even though countless scientists have tried.

One reason science has failed to take charge of religion is the scientific method can't determine whether God exists. The failure of scientists to verify God's existence was revealed in a 2009 poll by the Pew Research Center. This poll showed that scientists are almost evenly split over the belief in God, with 52% of scientists believing in God or a higher power and 41% not believing in either.

Although science has altered religion by proving that the Earth revolves around the sun and life evolved from amino acids, science is still unable to prove if there is a God, a Heaven, or a higher purpose to life. That's because God, Heaven, and any higher purpose to life are beyond the instruments and mathematical proofs of science. This means that some beliefs will always remain conjecture. However, by gaining a better understanding of our universe, we might put more logic and less emotion into our assumptions about God's intentions.

Science has also failed to solve our political disagreements because science can't determine what constitutes the ideal society. There are two reasons for this. One is that every person has a different concept of the ideal society. The other reason is every society has some problems, so there isn't an ideal society for scientists to experiment on.

What scientists have discovered by studying people in small business organizations is that people in supportive environments are capable of higher levels of accomplishment. A 2015 study by Frontiers in Psychology found that high levels of workplace stress can lead to several negative personal and performance outcomes. These finding are fairly intuitive and they reveal something that isn't too surprising: that the ideal society is one where we support each other and avoid engaging in negative emotions. Yet because of downsizing, outsourcing, and mergers, many employees are experiencing the negative emotions of anxiety, apprehension, cynicism, and fear, which leads to decreases in work performance.

Scientists have evidence that the ideal society is one where we all support each other. Unfortunately, business owners often profit from policies that harm their employees. This is why politics is so contentious: we're not all interested in supporting each other.

In theory, the ideal society is one where everyone shares in the community's ideas, profits, and labor. This seems to be a socialistic society. Yet socialism is a failed experiment in the real world because many people don't want to work, while many others don't want to share their profit and power. That's why capitalism is said to be better at coping with human nature.

Of course, capitalism isn't a panacea either because everyone pursuing their own self-interest has failed to create harmonious, just, and ecologically sound societies. This is why capitalism has been called, "The best of a bunch of bad ideologies." But our ideologies aren't the problem. The problem is human nature, or the problem is human nature is less than ideal.

We've failed to create an ideal society, not because we can't figure out what is fair, but because our impulses and emotions make it difficult for us to do what we know in our hearts and minds is fair. Unfortunately, it's difficult for many people to do what their intellect, conscience, and religion tell them because we have deeper and stronger motivations coming from our instincts.

If humans were blank slates who lacked instinctive motivations, then it would be easy to shape society with advice from science and religion. On the other hand, if humans were noble savages who were all born diligent, compassionate, and conscientious, then we wouldn't need a religion or an ideology to shape society. Indeed, we wouldn't need a government and its police, prisons, and armies if everyone lacked impulses or if everyone naturally behaved in an ideal manner. Yet we have always needed police and prisons and our religions and ideologies have continually failed to create healthy, crime-free societies because our instinctive impulses have always made it difficult for people to behave in ways that benefit society and their own health.

If humans were blank slates or noble savages, then it would be easy to stop people from stealing simply by telling them that stealing is wrong. Yet even though every major religion teaches that stealing is wrong and even though every society threatens those who steal with prison, there is a seemingly endless stream of blue and white-collar criminals.

Because most white-collar criminals are powerful enough, wealthy enough, and educated enough to escape prosecution, their damage to society is difficult to calculate. We can only speculate on how many billions of dollars are lost due to the frauds on Wall Street and to the waste in government. Even Donald Rumsfeld, the Secretary of Defense under George W. Bush admitted the day before 9/11, "According to some estimates we cannot track $2.3 trillion in transactions."

The only losses from crime that we can track are the losses due to smaller "blue collar" crimes like shoplifting, car theft, home burglary, and so on. The cost of shoplifting is about 12 billion a year, car theft is about 5 billion a year, and home burglary is about 3 billion a year. Of course, these numbers are nothing compared to the trillions of dollars lost each year due to the waste in government and the frauds on Wall Street. However, the cost of just one blue collar crime: shoplifting was enough for Consumers Reports to calculate that consumers pay higher prices in a sort of "crime tax" of $450.00 per family per year. One can only cringe to think how much each family is paying for all the trillions of "unknown" white collar crimes.

Also needed to create an ideal society is a world filled with healthy people. Yet even though people are continually bombarded with information about what is healthy, our healthcare system must cope with the fact that 40% of Americans are obese, 17% smoke cigarettes, and 9% are abusing or are dependent on drugs, alcohol, or both. Even though everyone must know that it's unsafe and illegal to drink alcohol and drive, our society must cope with the fact that 28 people die each day from drunk drivers, while an additional 720 people are left with serious injuries.

How can we create an ideal society when so many Americans are seriously damaging their own health and when so many are stealing from the government, industry, and taxpayers? The first step is to acknowledge that the battle isn't between our religions and ideologies; it's between our instincts and our conscience.

It's amazing how many people believe that their religion and/or political ideology could instantly change the world, as if their religion or political ideology instantly could stop people from stealing, taking drugs, and eating junk food. As if our world would be free of crime, drugs, pollution, and junk food if everyone was a Democrat, a Republican, a Christian, or some other religious and political affiliation. As if any idea in our head could instantly and completely eliminate our body's short-sighted and self-centered impulses.

Although millions of people continue to believe that their religion or political ideology can change the world, there has never been an idea or even a police force that could stop people from stealing, abusing drugs, eating junk food, trashing the environment, or texting and driving. Certainly, if everyone had an iron-will and if everyone fully embraced a religion of compassion and an ideology of healthful living, then our world would be a better place. But people don't have iron-wills, nor are people sitting around waiting for a religion or ideology to tell them how to behave. Instead, humans are born with powerful instinctive desires that cannot be easily pushed aside. Again, this is why our religions need to understand evolution: because our conscience is most often in conflict with our instincts.

Our instincts did not evolve to be a weak or a secondary source of motivation. Quite the reverse, our instincts evolved to be our primary source of motivation because humans and all other animals are born ignorant and, thus, are unable to consciously determine how to survive.

Without instinct, newborn animals wouldn't be motivated to find food, keep warm, or stay safe. Moreover, even mature animals need instincts to constantly monitor their temperature and energy levels so they don't overexert themselves. Yet all animals, including humans can survive just fine without religion or culture.

Humans are not born as blank slates waiting for culture to tell them how to behave, nor are we born as noble savages who naturally behave ethically. Instead, we are born as instinct-driven predators who can develop our compassion or give in to the selfish, impulsive, and short-sighted instincts we inherited from the lower animals.

Although our religions and ideologies can help us control our negative impulses, our religions and ideologies can also encourage war, racism, and despotism. Obviously, we need more than just a religion or ideology. We also need a conscience that is strong enough to keep our instincts from corrupting our religion or ideology.

Our religions and ideologies are weak because they must be embraced. Yet our instincts are powerful because they come preinstalled. Furthermore, our religions and ideologies are easily abandoned, while our instinctive impulses never leave us alone.

It's naive to assume that everyone's conscience is so strong and so compliant that our religions only need to state what is healthy and fair to get everyone to do what is healthy and fair. In reality, to do what's right, we need to control powerful inborn impulses, and that is easier said than done.

To create a perfect society, we don't need to find the perfect religion or the perfect ideology; we need to find perfect people. Yet it isn't so easy to find perfect people.

What is easy is to judge people by the beliefs they proclaim. Yet these proclamations mean little. This is what Josef Stalin's daughter said after defecting to America in 1967: "There aren't any capitalists or communists, there are just good and bad human beings."

Anyone can claim to be a capitalist or a communist just as anyone can claim to be a Christian or a Muslim, but every society is only as good as the people who make up that society. This is true of every society whether it's a small family or a large government, religion, or corporation. Unfortunately, every society is susceptible to monopolies of power and corruption of its leaders regardless of that society's religious and political beliefs because humans are all driven by shortsighted and self-centered impulses.

The main reason capitalism is more successful than communism is because communism relies on people working together, while capitalism relies more on individual self-interest. But we shouldn't be proud that capitalism is more successful that communism because this only shows that it's easier to motivate people with self-interest than compassion.

We're not fighting republicans, democrats, communists, capitalists, or some foreign ideology. We're fighting the unsavory elements in human nature. We're fighting greed, pride, anger, fear, laziness, jealousy, gluttony, and so on. Yet we argue about the waste, fraud, and corruption in government and industry as if crime was just an ideological mistake and not a failure of the will. As if all the blue and white-collar criminals were just ignorant of the law or unaware that their actions were hurting others. As if we only need to point out that greed, pride, anger, and jealousy are wrong to stop people from engaging in those behaviors.

Although most governments are now a mixture of socialism and capitalism, this isn't because scientists have figured out how we should mix socialism with capitalism. It's because the business sector has shown that it won't take care of the poor, sick, and elderly, while the government sector has shown that it can't respond to the rapidly changing market place. It's because socialism has proved to be an unattainable goal, while capitalism has proved to be an inequitable process so we are forced to temper the idealism of socialism with the pragmatism of capitalism.

After all the failed attempts to make either socialism or capitalism fair and equitable, you would think that everyone would agree that there are no simple solutions to getting people to live and work together. And yet, we aren't united by the difficulty of overcoming our self-centered impulses because too many people want a simpler answer.

Too many people want to complain about socialism and capitalism, as if one ideology or the other really could create an ideal society. As if life truly had a simple answer, but all the previous generations just failed to see it.

It's no great achievement to point out how free markets can lead to monopolies or how government regulations can stifle progress. The challenge is to explain how any ideology can force everyone in government and industry to be honest, diligent, healthy, and compassionate. The challenge is to explain how any idea in our head can eliminate the shortsighted impulses that surge through our body.

Religion and politics are filled with fanatics because millions of people want to believe that there is a simple solution to our problems. Millions, if not billions of people want to believe that an ideology, a savior, an extraterrestrial, or a harmonic convergence will transform society, while only a small minority are willing to accept that everyone must constantly struggle to control their own negative impulses and emotions.

Society can't change overnight because humans can't easily control their impulses and emotions. Society has always and will always change slowly as the number of individuals who learn to control their negative impulses and emotions slowly increases. Unfortunately, as each new generation is born, the struggle to rise above one's short-sighted impulses and emotions starts all over again.

Luckily, each generation inherits laws and codes of conduct that encourage higher behavior from the previous generation. Yet each generation also inherits instincts and impulses that push them towards easy and self-serving behaviors. That's why the battle between our higher aspirations and lower impulses will never end.

What's that cliché? "Life is complex, but people want simple answers." This isn't a minor issue or a pearl of wisdom that needs to be tossed out now and again. This is the primary reason we're unable to unite and solve our problems.

If everyone wanted their life to be filled with complex challenges, then we would all come together and confront our problems. But the threats of nuclear war, environmental destruction, and economic inequality are only getting worse because too many people want simple answers.

Too many people want to be entertained and amused, not challenged by the complexity of running a world where over 7 billion semi-domesticated predatory animals are all fighting for their own wants. That's why polls continually show that most people know more about the entertainment industry than their own government.

The desire for an easy life has turned religion and politics into a charade. The charade is that our religious and political leaders have simple answers to our problems. Unfortunately, our religious and political leaders aren't the only ones pretending, as the masses must also feign a belief in simple answers for this show to go on.

The authorities in one religion are dismissed by the believers of the other religions and the authorities in one political party are rejected by the followers of the other political parties because the authorities don't have all the answers. All the authorities have are partial answers, which wouldn't be a problem if everyone was willing to accept that life is too complicated for anyone to have the final solution. Unfortunately, most people will respond only to simple, absolute answers no matter how absurd and divisive those answers are.

The scientific community is also hindered by our desire for simple answers because scientific facts are also disputed when they conflict with simpler beliefs. This is primarily why evolution is still denied: it conflicts with the simpler story of creationism. This is also why global warming is denied: it conflicts with simpler business plans.

It's often claimed that the masses are uniformed because the media is withholding information and that "all we have to do" is give people the right information. But the alternative media is everywhere. Unfortunately, the alternative media is usually underfunded and ignored because most people prefer the simpler stories on commercial radio and TV.

It's flattering and it's optimistic, but it's naive to assume that learning is a universal human goal and that the solution to all of our problems is to simply provide people with the correct information. Unfortunately, life is so complex and challenging that a majority of people will always prefer simple stories over knowledge.

Having an open mind is a challenge because we live in an infinitely complex universe that stretches out endlessly in all directions. This is why so many people in the past were mad at Galileo and why so many people today prefer the charlatans in religion, politics, and the mass-media: most people don't want to be shown how complex our universe is.

Most people will accept only simple answers even though our infinite universe can't possibly have a simple answer. In fact, our universe can be only partially explained by some extremely complex theories. That's why we must help people become comfortable with complex, open-ended ideas in religion, politics, and science.

To unite our world, we must help people find peace with the endless quest for knowledge and self-improvement that is our lot. We must reveal the absurdity in all the simple answers and increase the affection for learning that the late Isaac Asimov so eloquently expressed in this statement: "It would be terrible to know everything because there would be nothing left to learn."

A life without mental, physical, emotional, and spiritual challenges is a lesser life. In fact, a life without any challenges is unpleasant. That's why we create puzzles, engage in sports, and play games. Unfortunately, our desire to find the easiest route to pleasure continually pushes people towards the simplest of challenges.

Although most people impulsively turn away from the difficulties in our world, our brain will atrophy without challenges, so if we truly care about our health, then we will rejoice like Isaac Asimov that there will always be more complicated puzzles to solve.

It doesn't matter if life doesn't have a simple solution. What matters is our universe is logical. What matters is that we can understand and unite behind this logic.

Hopefully, this book will reveal the logic in the material world, human behavior, and God, or in science, politics, and religion. Hopefully, by understanding the logic in the material world, human behavior, and God, we can make better decisions about our physical health, about what other people will do, and about what God wants from us.

Chapter Nine

Suffering

Every religion has struggled to explain why God allows innocent people to suffer. Basically, the Western, or Abrahamic religions see suffering as a test of one's faith, as evidence that God works in mysterious ways, and as punishment for Adam and Eve disobeying God in the Garden of Eden, while the Eastern, or Indian religions see suffering as the result of karma and our attachment to worldly and impermanent things.

Atheists also try to explain undeserved suffering and many insist that suffering is proof that God doesn't exist. As Michael Shermer, publisher of Skeptic magazine and columnist for Scientific American wrote in response to the US House of Representatives voting in 2011 to reaffirm the national motto "In God We Trust,"

> If you think that God is watching over the U.S., please ask yourself why he glanced away during 9/11 or why he chose to abandon the good folks of New Orleans during Hurricane Katrina, and why he continues to allow earthquakes and cancers to strike down even blameless children: The problem of evil--why bad things happen to good people if an all-powerful and all-good God is in control of things--has haunted the faithful since it was first articulate millenniums ago, with nigh a solution on the horizon.

In order to plan for our life, we must figure out if atheists or one of the world's religions is correct. We must decide who is giving good advice and who is giving bad advice. We may also decide that neither atheism nor any of the present religions is adequately explaining our world and that we need to find another philosophy to base our life on.

Of course, the point of this book is that we need a better explanation of life because atheism and the present religions have failed to unite us. The point is that our beliefs must move forward before they can bring us together.

Although millions of people claim that everything they need to know about God and the world was revealed by their ancient prophets, this is like claiming that everything we need to know about the human body was explained by some ancient doctor. Obviously, no intelligent person would go to a doctor whose beliefs about the human body were hundreds or thousands of years old. In fact, no intelligent person would go to a doctor whose practice isn't completely up-to-date. And yet, millions of people continue to embrace religions whose ideas are hundreds or thousands of years old, as if our understanding of God was complete even though our understanding of the human body isn't. As if God was easier to understand than the things he created.

There are so many errors in the world's religions that it's absurd to believe that any religion is infallible. But it's also wrong to take the opposite approach that all religions are without merit. Unfortunately, there is rarely any rational or middle ground when religion is discussed.

Few people would claim that Aristotle was completely right or completely wrong because most people accept that mortals can't fully understand the universe. And yet, our religions are most commonly discussed as if they were either infallible, or complete junk.

If any religion truly was the word of God, then we would all know it because that religion would be so accurate as to be indisputable. But like the Greek philosophies, the world's religions all contain errors because they too are mortal creations.

Even though the traditional religions offer some good advice, this advice is overly simplistic, mostly outdated, and continually polluted by xenophobic, authoritarian, and doomsday declarations. This isn't to say that people shouldn't read the classics or study the traditional religions, but that we should read and study them to understand what little our ancestors could discern about their world.

Religion isn't just about God; it's also about people. In fact, the traditional religions are more about the hopes, desires, and frustrations of ancient peoples than they are about God.

Another problem with old books, whether they deal with religion, philosophy, or science is they are filled with simplistic and often erroneous ideas. This forces the reader to sort through piles of rubbish to gain a few scraps of wisdom. In contrast, most modern books have the naïve and erroneous ideas winnowed out so the reader has an easier time finding useful information. Unfortunately, many people read only for a diversion and you can't have your mind diverted away from reality by a book that is filled with clear and concise ideas. That's why so many modern books are purposely filled with fluff.

It should be obvious that the beliefs of past theologians, philosophers, and scientists are unavoidably naive. To put it another way, it should be obvious that humanity's beliefs are constantly evolving.

If everyone accepted that our knowledge is evolving, then our religions would be easier to advance. But if the world's religions were seen as evolving mortal creations, then they would lose much of their appeal because they would no longer be seen as magical, privileged, and complete knowledge.

Most religions are not marketed as evolving branches of knowledge because that isn't what most people want to buy. What most people want are simple answers in an entertaining social setting.

Most religions are franchises, or most are just slight variations on a similar business model. And although it might seem harmless that most religions are selling simple answers amid family-orientated entertainment, it's disastrous when the major religions are just more tax-evading corporations preying on the desires of self-absorbed consumers.

When a religion becomes a business, all challenging truths are pushed aside so the owners can maximize profit. Of course, a capitalist might argue that the market will ensure that the most popular religions are offering the most accurate knowledge. But that is like saying the market will ensure that the most popular restaurants are offering the best nutrition. Regrettably, popularity doesn't signify that a restaurant is healthy or that a religion is accurate.

Unfortunately, we live in a world where all good things, like exercise, learning, sobriety, and healthful eating are difficult, while all bad things, like laziness, ignorance, drug use, and unhealthful eating are easy. Unfortunately, in a world where easy is bad for you and difficult is good for you, popularity will not signify accuracy. Instead, popularity will signify easy, unhealthy, and inaccurate.

The most popular beliefs and behaviors are not necessarily the best beliefs and behaviors. More likely, they are just the simplest and most entertaining beliefs and behaviors. This is why the theory of evolution has historically been less popular than the story of creationism: 6 days of creation is easier to hear about than 4 billion years of evolution.

Science is more complicated than religion because science isn't shaped by what the masses want to hear. Science is shaped by the experimental evidence. Yet the lack of evidence for God allows people to judge the world's religions solely by how popular and entertaining they are.

Another challenge of trying to advance our religions is there are too many religions to advance. First of all, there are 11 major religions that each have over 7 million followers. They are the Baha'i faith, Buddhism, Christianity, Confucianism, Hinduism, Islam, Jainism, Judaism, Shinto, Sikhism, and Taoism. There are also 9 smaller religions that each have between 1 and 3 million followers. And if we want to be fair and consider all the religions with less than 1 million followers, we would have to examine and discuss thousands of different religions.

Obviously, it's impossible to discuss a thousand different religions and still have time to discuss anything else. Yet even if we tried to discuss only the most popular religion: Christianity, there are 3 main branches of Christianity: Catholic, Orthodox, and Protestant. Not only do these 3 branches disagree, but there are over 30 smaller denominations within these branches. With all these competing denominations, whatever is said about Christianity could be disputed by another Christian, so we could never agree on and, thus, decide how to advance even this one religion.

Who gets to decide if Christians accept homosexuality and women clergy? Similarly, who gets to define what karma is? Although many people have tried to control what each religion stands for, anyone who disagrees with the established definition is free to start their own denomination.

Imagine if geology had thousands of contradictory denominations. Imagine if we were all free to create our own "geology." Luckily, the sciences are easy to discuss because the disagreements are only over the frontiers and not about the fundamentals.

The sciences are easy to discuss because scientists have agreed on the fundamental laws that govern our universe. To advance religion, we must also develop a consensus on what is fundamentally true about God.

Here are just a few reasons why only a brief description of the world's religions will be given here. First, none of the world's religions are universally accepted. Second, none of the world's religions have fixed definitions. Third, none of the world's religions have proven to be infallible. Fourth, the world's religions need to be critiqued and advanced, not defined and enshrined.

To begin our short critique of the world's beliefs, we must start with the simplest belief. And the simplest belief is actually atheism because a world without a God is simpler than a world with a God.

A world without a God is simple because it's one-dimensional. It's just a material world. This makes life easy for atheists because they don't need to worry about the desires of a higher being. Atheists only need to worry about their own desires and, at times, the desires of people who are close to them.

Life would be simpler if the material world was all there was and our spirit, consciousness, and free will were illusions. This would simplify life because we wouldn't need to develop our spirit and intellect for a future existence, nor would we need to worry about there being any spiritual consequences to our actions. But life doesn't appear to be that simple, which is one reason why atheism has failed to unite us.

Polls consistently show that about 90% of Americans believe in God. Although 90% of Americans could be wrong, with such a large percentage of people believing in God, we must consider the possibility that life is more than just a chemical reaction. This isn't to say that we must accept one of the established religions, but we should consider the possibility that life is too complex for science and materialism to fully explain.

Although atheists like to point out how the world's religions are full of errors, con-artists, and gullible people, the errors and even the criminality in religion doesn't prove that God doesn't exist. It only proves that many people are naive, while many others are unscrupulous.

Regardless of how many problems exist within the organized religions, our life may still be obstructed by more than just the laws of physics and our own biology because God may also have plans that interfere with our dreams. In fact, it may be foolish to dismiss God because he may hamper our ambitions far more than all the physical laws that science can reveal to us.

Atheists also like to point out how God appears to be absent because he doesn't protect us from crime, disease, and natural disasters. However, bad things happening to good people also doesn't prove that God doesn't exist. It may only prove that God doesn't want to remove all challenges from our life.

If God protected us from every danger, then we wouldn't need to think about our actions. For example, we wouldn't need to worry about driving while intoxicated because God would always keep us from crashing. We also wouldn't need to worry about our diet, sexual behaviors, and environmental impacts because God would make sure that no harm came from those challenges either. Such a sheltered and insulated world might seem desirable, but a world without any consequences to our actions wouldn't make sense.

Even Michael Shermer's question of why, "God allows earthquakes and cancers to strike down even blameless children" evades the real question, which is, "What are you going to do to help cure cancer and make buildings more earthquake resistant?" The real question is, "Should our cancer researchers and earthquake engineers just throw up their hands and walk away from their jobs because they are doing God's work?"

This is the hypocrisy of atheism: atheists criticize theists for being anti-intellectual, and yet, many atheists expect God to babysit us. And because God doesn't protect us from all crime, disease, and natural disasters, many atheists claim that this proves God doesn't exist. As if atheists couldn't imagine a God who would challenge them and expect self-reliance. As if atheists could imagine only an indulgent, doting God, or no God at all.

Another desire of atheists is to have scientific proof of God's existence. Yet expecting God to prove his existence is similar to expecting your boss, teacher, or parents to always prove when they are watching. It's far more logical that God would stay hidden so he can see how we act when we think no one is watching.

People will alter their behavior when they think someone is watching. This is especially true when someone with power and authority is watching. Yet many atheists feel that God should make it obvious if he exists, as if that wouldn't alter our behavior, or as if God would want to force our behavior.

Do you want companions who you have to constantly watch over and who you have to constantly punish and reward to achieve good behavior? Of course not, we all want companions who are honest and kind even when we aren't looking. Yet many atheists seem mystified that God would want what we want: people who are honest and kind on their own. Many atheists seem to think that God would prefer people who he has to constantly punish and reward even though we want to be around people who do the right thing even if we don't punish or reward them.

Instead of rejecting God because he doesn't protect us from all dangers, make his existence obvious, and force everyone to be good, maybe atheists should consider why God would want us to struggle with our conscience and act on our own initiatives. Maybe atheists should consider that God lets us deal with life's challenges on our own for the same reason that all good teachers, coaches, and parents make their students, athletes, and children figure out how to deal with life's challenges on their own: it builds character.

It's easy to prove that the God we desire doesn't exist because it's easy to prove that God doesn't protect us from every danger, make his aspirations clear, and force everyone to be good. But this doesn't prove that the God we don't desire doesn't exist because it doesn't prove that the God who wants us to think and learn and take care of ourselves doesn't exist.

God may also not reveal himself because he may not be a physical being who can appear on our doorstep. God may just be a consciousness or he may be the universe itself. God may be all around us and within us, so the only way he may be able to reveal himself to us is by altering something in our surroundings, like the weather.

Perhaps someday, both atheists and theists will agree that there are few simple answers in science or religion. Perhaps someday, we will accept that an infinite universe and an infinite God cannot be fully explained because they can be only partially understood.

The next simplest belief after atheism also isn't an organized religion. It's the belief that God is neutral. This belief is only slightly more complex than atheism because if God is neutral, then we may want to consider his existence, but, like atheists, we don't need to worry about how he might interfere with our life or judge us for things we do.

A neutral or impersonal God is simple because such a being would not add another layer of complexity to our world. An impersonal God would stay out of our life, so there would be little reason to contemplate or worry about him.

Strangely, the two simplest beliefs are associated with the most complex human endeavor: science, because polls show that 41% of scientists don't believe in God while 45% reject the idea of a personal God. This is in contrast to the mere 8% of the general public who don't believe in God and the 25% who reject the idea of a personal God.

The rejection of a personal God was something that Albert Einstein was adamant about. At a symposium on Science, Philosophy, and Religion in 1941, Einstein made his feelings clear that science could not accept: "a deity who could meddle at whim in the events of his creation or in the lives of his creatures." Einstein, like many other Europeans and like Thomas Jefferson and Benjamin Franklin, felt that "a spirit is manifest in the laws of the universe," but that this God does not meddle in our daily affairs.

Einstein felt that the laws of nature were immutable. This is probably because, like most scientists, Einstein saw that the world was logical and predictable.

It's difficult to understand how the world could remain logical and predictable if God is constantly intervening in our world. It would seem that if God is intervening in our world, then our world would change in erratic and unpredictable ways. This is probably why more scientists than laypeople are atheists or believe that God is neutral: because more scientists than laypeople see experimental evidence that the world is logical and predictable. Of course, God may be intelligent enough to intervene in his creation and still leave the laws of physics intact for us.

Scientists are correct that God appears to be neutral because our world doesn't change in erratic and unpredictable ways. But arguing that God is neutral because the world is governed by stable laws assumes that God couldn't fool a mortal. It assumes that a being who is capable of creating a universe that is infinite in size and complexity couldn't intervene in our world without a scientist detecting it.

Perhaps God is smarter than we are. Sounds logical and it seems like something that most people would accept, but most people act like God is a fool. For example, most religious people act like God is just a dimwitted, insecure bureaucrat whose only concern is that we worship him and engage in the proper rituals. On the other side, many scientists assume that God is so inept that he couldn't intervene in his creation without them knowing about it.

It's understandable why many scientists want proof of God's existence just as it's understandable why many religious people want to influence God with rituals, sayings, and worship. It's also understandable why many religious people would want God to take care of them just as it's understandable why many scientists would want God to stay out of their life altogether. But it isn't logical that God will do what most people want. What's logical is that God has more challenging aspirations than most people have.

Although many scientists claim that God is neutral, far more people believe that God is not neutral and that the laws of physics are not immutable. But the real question is whether we have the ability to determine if God is intervening in our world.

Perhaps we could examine our life and see if it unfolds in a random, or a purposeful way. Of course, the mind often sees patterns where there are none, so we must be careful to determine if the events in our life are random occurrences, or if they shape our life in a way that God would find desirable. But to answer that question we must first answer this question: "What sort of life would God find desirable?"

Perhaps most people have trouble understanding God because their idea of a desirable life is different than God's idea of a desirable life. Perhaps most people desire an easy life devoid of challenges, and so they are confused and claim that, "God doesn't exist," or that "God acts in mysterious ways" when life keeps challenging them. Perhaps if more people desired a challenging life, then more people would see God in their life.

Claiming that God is neutral is similar to claiming that God doesn't exist because a neutral God would have no more effect on our life than a nonexistent God. This is probably why Einstein was called an atheist even though he expressed a belief in, "a God who reveals himself in the lawful harmony of all that exists:" because a belief in a neutral God is not what most people considered a belief in God.

If we conclude, as Einstein did, that, "God is not concerned with the fate and the doings of mankind," then we should not plan for any help or any hindrance from God. In fact, we no longer need to discuss God if we believe that he is neutral because a neutral God will play no part in our life. All we need to understand are how the laws of physics and biology shape our life, which is a much simpler discussion. However, if we believe that God is intervening in our world, then we must determine what motivates God to intervene. We must continue with our quest to solve that great religious question, "Why would a concerned and involved God allow for so much suffering?"

Most Eastern, or Indian religions also reject the idea of a personal God and teach that suffering is the result of karma and our attachment to worldly and impermanent things. Basically, the Eastern religions claim that suffering can be eliminated only when we escape from the endless cycle of birth and death and enter Nirvana.

If we don't believe the atheists who claim that we should plan for a purely material world and if we don't believe the scientists who claim that we should plan for a completely neutral God, then perhaps we should plan for the world to dispense with karma. Perhaps we should accept that suffering is the result of our craving for worldly and impermanent things.

Certainly, we shouldn't cling to impermanent things, but humanity wouldn't exist if we all lived like monks and nuns who had no possessions and no children. This is the main problem with seeking a cessation to suffering: an absolute cessation isn't possible as long as we are part of the cycle of birth and death.

Life is impermanent, which means that life is imperfect. But escaping from the cycle of birth and death is not a solution for most people. That's why the Third Noble Truth of Buddhism should not claim that a "cessation to suffering is possible," but that there is only a way to "reduce suffering."

The Eastern religions are correct that we should reduce our craving for material things and increase our compassion for other living things, but we mortals can't live a totally blameless life because our very existence demands resources that other creatures need. Again, the problem is not in the attempt to reduce suffering, it's in the belief that there is a complete solution to life besides leaving the cycle of life.

Most people want to be part of the cycle of life. Yet to live, we must clear land for our farms, roads, houses, stores, schools, and so on. Unfortunately, we can't clear land without causing harm to all the creatures living on that land.

Although many monks and nuns survive by charity and even though some monks and nuns refuse to leave their monastery for fear of trampling on living things, even these austere lives don't result in a totally blameless existence because the maintenance of the monastery and the production of food, clothing, and utensils that supports those in monastery still causes harm and destroys animal habitat.

Even if we are not the ones building the roads and building or producing and shipping our food, clothing, and utensils, as long as we inhabit a physical body, we will cause harm because our mere existence increases the number of roads, buildings, foods, clothing, and utensils that must be produced, built, or shipped. Moreover, the attempt to live like hermits so we might avoid causing harm actually does cause harm because humanity needs everyone to participate.

Although many monks and nuns do participate in society, there is a desire among many religious people to silence their thoughts, renounce life, and separate themselves from society. This causes harm because it leaves less good people to deal with the psychopaths, sociopaths, and narcissists living among us. Unfortunately, if the psychopaths, sociopaths, and narcissists are not confronted, then they will create even more harm.

Studies show that about 1% of people are psychopaths, 4% are sociopaths, and 6% are narcissists. This means that about 11% of people either lack or have a diminished conscience and ability for compassion. This is why our religions must not encourage people to silence their mind, retreat from society, and treat everyone with loving kindness: 11% of people have no qualms about harming others to get what they want.

As long as there are substantial numbers of psychopaths, sociopaths, and narcissists in our world, we will need police, prisons, and even armies. We will need good people who are willing to confront these self-centered individuals and treat them as we would not want to be treated.

Although the Eastern religions are correct that there will be less suffering in our world when we reduce our cravings for impermanent, material things, there is also less suffering in our world because of modern medicine and technology. And modern medicine and technology exist only because science focuses on the impermanent material world.

There is less suffering in birth, sickness, aging, and even the process of death because of Western medicine and technology. This doesn't imply that the Eastern religions are wrong about the mind's role in suffering, but that we need to alter our religious beliefs as we learn more about the physical and biological causes of suffering. And the 14th Dali Lama fully embraced this belief in this statement:

"If science proves some belief of Buddhism wrong, then Buddhism will have to change. In my view, science and Buddhism share a search for the truth and for understanding reality. By learning from science about aspects of reality where its understanding may be more advanced, I believe that Buddhism enriches its own worldview."

The Eastern religions are also correct that life is constantly changing and that this impermanence causes suffering. However, a world without change would be even more insufferable. This is something that has been pointed out many times: Heaven and Nirvana, or endless bliss would be endless monotony. It's also been pointed out that change is what makes life an adventure. Yet even though it's difficult to say anything that hasn't been said before, we still aren't united by the understanding that our world is the best of all possible worlds.

Even though most people enjoy the change of seasons and even though most people enjoy the fact that there is always something new around the corner, few religions acknowledge that life can't be an adventure without also having the disadvantages brought about by change. Unfortunately, the major religions either see life's impermanence as a flaw or as punishment for Eve being tricked by the devil instead of explaining how change is necessary to make life meaningful and challenging.

Life isn't suffering; it's challenging. This is evidenced by the fact that the primary way we have reduced suffering is by understanding and overcoming life's challenges.

To determine if the Eastern religions are correct about karma, we must first decide if our karmic rewards and punishments come in this life, or another life. We must decide if karma affects us immediately, or in some future life that we cannot see.

If our karmic rewards and punishments won't appear until our next life, then our world and any God or Gods will seem neutral because this world won't show any reaction to our actions. This view of karma won't be verifiable, which means it won't be something we can plan for or unite behind. It will only be another source of hope and speculation, and the goal of this book isn't to offer more hope and speculation. My goal is to reveal spiritual and philosophical laws that we can all verify, agree on, and plan for.

The only type of karma we can verify is the karma that affects this life. This karma would be similar to the concept of "De" in Taoism and the Christian concept that we "reap what we sow."

If karma applies to this life and if we reap what we sow in this life, then we should be able to verify that the world, or that God is not neutral. We should be able to see that good people are growing stronger while selfish people are growing weaker.

Although there are many health benefits to being a compassionate person, there is also a health benefit to being wealthy and in not being a martyr or political prisoner. Unfortunately, fighting injustice can get you tortured, imprisoned, or killed, so most people should agree that, although we reap what we sow in many ways, we don't immediately, clearly, or absolutely reap what we sow. Most people should agree that if karma was clearly, absolutely, and immediately handed out, then everyone would work for social justice and only lunatics would do bad things.

Billions of sane people are doing self-centered things because we aren't clearly punished or clearly rewarded for our actions. Moreover, far too many tyrants have enjoyed long, luxurious lives and far too many wars, genocides, and natural disasters have affected children who were too young to have sown bad seeds to justify the belief in karma. Of course, this is why so many of those who believe in karma also claim that karma is carried over from a past life and into a future life. Yet the primary reason why the Eastern religions have failed to convince the skeptics and unite the world is most of us can't verify if some children are suffering because of their past life or if all tyrants will be punished in a future life. All that most of us can be sure of is that there isn't enough karma in this life.

It's impossible to verify, plan for, or even make sense of karma if we are punished and rewarded for a past life that we can't remember. Moreover, if people in the future who can't remember us will be punished and re-warded for our actions, then karma doesn't seem fair. Perhaps this is why karma is said to be a natural law and not an act of a divine being.

Although many people believe that there is some karma or some supernatural benefit to being a good person, karma can't be the primary law of this world because it doesn't explain why Hitler and Stalin were allowed to kill and torture all the millions of seemingly innocent people they killed and tortured. Similarly, karma can't be the prime directive of this world because it doesn't explain why the Chinese army was allowed to invade Tibet and kill so many of its Buddhist monks and destroy so many of its Buddhist monasteries.

To make sense, karma must come from a past life and go into a future life. But most of us can't verify if this view of karma is more than just a good story because most people are not aware of past lives. Most of us know only of this life, and in this life, karma isn't something we can verify, agree on, or plan for.

The belief in karma is controversial because there isn't clear justice in this life. This is why every country has some military and some criminal justice system: we can't expect karma to control crime just as we can't trust our karma to keep another country from invading.

Perhaps karma doesn't immediately right all wrongs because some other law is more powerful than the law of karma. Perhaps karma is just a secondary, or even a tertiary law. Perhaps we need to find another law that is immediately and clearly applied and, thus, is something we can all verify, agree on, and plan for.

A simplification of what the Western religions teach is that we suffer because of sin and because we inhabit a fallen world. Basically, the Western religions maintain that the only way out of suffering is when the messiah comes and those with the proper faith are taken to Heaven.

If we don't feel that it's wise to plan for no God, a neutral God, or karma, then perhaps we should plan for the messiah to soon arrive and bring this world to an end. Perhaps we should all prepare for the "end times" and for our generation to be the last generation, or perhaps this is just more comforting, but bad advice.

Because thousands of generations of Jews, Christians, and Muslims have fruitlessly waited for the end of the world, our generation can't logically count on the arrival of the messiah either. Instead, the belief in the end times appears to be just more hope and speculation that doesn't pan out.

Perhaps God doesn't want to destroy our world. Perhaps God likes the world just the way it is. It certainly makes more sense that the world is still here in spite of all the doomsday predictions because God likes what he created.

It also doesn't make sense that suffering exists because the devil tricked Adam and Eve into eating from the tree of knowledge, as the Western religions claim. What's makes sense is that God, and not the devil, is in control. Unfortunately, few people want life to be as complex and challenging as it is so they flock to religions that tell them why the world is unsatisfactory, or not as God wants it.

Both the Eastern and Western religions tell us that our world is flawed. Yet they also offer advice on how we should live. In that sense, the Eastern and Western religions have two sides to their teaching. One side explains why we suffer, such as, Adam and Eve being expelled from the Garden of Eden and the Four Noble Truths of Buddhism, which are, by nature, negative and the other side explains what we can do to lessen suffering, such as self-sacrifice and following the Noble Eightfold Path, which, of course, are more positive.

The messages from the Eastern and Western religions are mixed because they both disparage life and then offer a path to a better life. But this truly good life can't be realized until the rapture comes or until we escape from the cycle of birth and death. Unfortunately, this makes it difficult to know if we're supposed to work to improve our world, or if we're supposed to renounce our world and hope for its end.

It's difficult for many religious people to care about environmental degradation when they have renounced our world or when their religion tells them that our world is about to end. Similarly, it's difficult for many religious people to care about war, injustice, and corruption when such things are signs that our world is flawed and that the messiah will soon arrive. That's why mixed messages don't work and why our religions need to be clear if our world is a mistake, or if it's exactly as God wants it.

Of course, the major religions also have a negative slant on life because life was so difficult and our ability to lessen suffering was so limited back when the Eastern and Western religions were created. But, today, the proof of our ability to lessen suffering is everywhere and most people now enjoy life and don't want it or the world to end. Unfortunately, most religions continue to denounce life because they cater mainly to those who are nearing the end of life.

As we age and our passions start to fade, there is a desire to turn away from life. Moreover, once our best years are behind us, there is a desire to focus on another life. This is why so many religions disparage our desires and this world: because they cater mainly to the elderly who only want to think of another world.

If the world's religions focused more on the young than the elderly, then they would have to contend with the fact that the majority of young people don't want to hear about the end times or how they need to renounce their desires. They would have to accept that life is quite enjoyable for those who are young, healthy, and living in modern societies. Perhaps this is why the new age religions and the mega-churches are so positive: they were created in the modern era and they cater to a younger and more affluent segment of society than the traditional religions.

The traditional religions are too focused on explaining how our world is flawed because our world may not be flawed. It may be exactly as God wants it. This isn't to say that God wants our world to be filled with suffering and injustice, but that God wants our world to be filled with challenges. It's to say that God doesn't want us to live in an idyllic, carefree world like Heaven or Nirvana, but in an imperfect world that we must exert ourselves to understand and improve. It's to say that God created life's imperfections to motivate people. Unfortunately, most people are not motivated to improve our world because most religions are not clear if we are supposed to improve or renounce this world.

Chapter Ten

Laws

Science has reduced suffering more than the world's religions because science assumes that we can improve our world, while most religions insist that our world is fallen and hopelessly flawed. Science has also united humanity more than the world's religions because science gives us laws that we can test, verify, modify, and agree on, while most religions tell us stories that we can't test, verify, modify, or agree on.

Religious unity hasn't come from the traditional religions because they don't adequately explain the planet we live on, the universe that surrounds us, or the diverse people we interact with. Religious unity will come only when our religious beliefs make sense of the past and present and offers accurate predictions of the future.

Most people should understand our world well enough to make some predictions about what God intends our world to do. And the prediction I have tried to emphasize throughout this book is that God wants and, thus, God designed our world so it would be a constant challenge to everyone.

It might seem obvious that life is a constant challenge to everyone. But if we can find a higher purpose to these challenges, then we should be able to agree that God purposely designed life's challenges, and that would be a significant religious consensus. Moreover, the prediction that God designed life to be a purposeful challenge should replace all the unfulfilled predictions about karma, harmonic convergences, and messiahs arising to eliminate life's challenges.

Although many religious people and even many atheists believe that God should answer all our prayers and protect us from all dangers, if God did those things, then life wouldn't be a challenge. Moreover, if karma righted all wrongs, then life also wouldn't be a challenge. But no matter how much faith people have in prayer or karma, there is a more powerful law: the law that God wants life to always be a challenge.

Rather than putting our faith in karma or prayer, it's better to have faith that God will always challenge us. It's better to accept that God wants us to answer our own prayers and work to bring about the justice that we want karma to create. It's better to accept that prayer and karma are feeble laws compared to the law that God wants to challenge us. Lastly, it's better to understand that the most successful and contented individuals are those who want, expect, and enjoy life's constant emotional, intellectual, and spiritual challenges, while the most frustrated and unhappy people are those who want, expect, and strive for a life without any challenges.

It's easy to verify that life is a constant challenge to everyone because it's easy to verify how eating healthy foods is a constant challenge to everyone, how avoiding drugs is a constant challenge to everyone, how exercising is a constant challenge to everyone, how gaining wisdom is a constant challenge to everyone, and how controlling one's anger, pride, greed, jealousy, and other emotions are a constant challenge for everyone. Furthermore, it doesn't matter if you are young or old, rich or poor, wise or ignorant, life is still a constant challenge. Certainly, some of life's challenges are more strenuous to the young than the old, the poor than the rich, and the ignorant than the wise, but it's impossible to find anyone who isn't constantly challenged by the daily demands of life.

Of course, atheists might argue that it's only the laws of physics that make exercising, healthy eating, avoiding drugs, gaining knowledge, and controlling one's emotions a constant challenge. But this is precisely why this law is fundamental and universal: everyone should be able to agree that life is a constant challenge whether they believe in God or not. The only reason for faith is the belief that life's challenges lead to some intangible, spiritual benefit or a reward in some future life.

No faith is needed to accept that life is a constant challenge to everyone because it's easy to verify how obtaining fresh, healthy foods is a constant challenge to everyone. Yet the rich seem to falsify this law because they don't need to struggle to acquire fresh, healthy foods. However, the rich are still constantly challenged to eat healthy foods instead of junk-foods.

The rich are not challenged in the same ways that poor people are challenged. But the rich are still constantly challenged because their wealth allows for idleness and excess.

Idleness and excess are not minor challenges, especially in a world where every type of junk food and every type of legal and illegal drug temps us. In fact, studies have shown that as a society grows more prosperous, both obesity rates and drug use go up. This is verified by the rise in obesity rates in China and India and by the "increase in heroin consumption in East Africa, the rise of cocaine addiction in West Africa and South America, and the surge in the production and abuse of synthetic drugs in the Middle East and South-East Asia," as cited by the United Nations Office on Drugs and Crime.

Numerous studies have shown that people with higher incomes are more likely to use both legal and illegal drugs. As Jennifer Warner wrote on WebMD, "The use of drugs seems to be a feature of more affluent countries."

Although wealth does make life less challenging in many respects, not having to work is a challenge in itself because work supplies purpose, a sense of accomplishment, and something to do besides taking drugs. More importantly, wealth doesn't do anything to eliminate the emotional and spiritual challenges of overcoming anger, pride, greed, jealousy, gluttony, laziness, and so on.

Experiments by Paul Piff and his colleagues at the University of California, Berkeley, found that wealthy people actually find it more challenging to experience compassion than people with lower incomes. It appears that wealth is so insulating that it reduces one's ability to relate to the circumstances of less fortunate people.

Although wealth eliminates many of life's challenges, it doesn't eliminate the challenge of becoming a healthy, caring, and compassionate person, which, if there is a God, is the main challenge of life. Certainly, wealth alters life's challenges and wealth offers a set of challenges that many of us dream of, but not having to work and having excess money is still a challenge.

Another fundamental law that we should all be able to agree on is that life's challenges force everyone to prove who they are. This law is also fundamental because no other law can falsify or supersede it. For example, if God answered all our prayers, then we wouldn't have to prove what we are willing to do to provide for ourselves. Similarly, if karma righted all wrongs, then we wouldn't have to prove what we are willing to do to combat life's injustices. But prayer and karma don't eliminate life's challenges and, thus, they don't allow us to avoid proving whether we are lazy or tenacious, cowardly or courageous, indifferent or compassionate.

Of course, atheists might argue that they are only proving to themselves and those close to them who they are, while everyone else is incorrectly assuming that they are also proving to God whether they are lazy or tenacious, cowardly or courageous, indifferent or compassionate. But, once again, it doesn't matter if you believe in God or not. What matters is we can all agree that life is a constant stream of challenges that continually forces everyone to prove who they are. The only reason for faith is if you want to believe that God rewards or punishes us in some intangible way or in some future life for what we prove about ourselves in this life.

Although we can't verify what happens after death, it's easy to verify how our unavoidable quest for food, or how our unavoidable quest to obtain money to buy food proves who we are today. Yet, once again, it seems that the rich falsify this law because they don't need to be employed. But even the idle rich are constantly proving who they are by how they spend, donate, and invest their money.

It doesn't matter if you work or not, you constantly prove who you are by how you spend, donate, and invest whatever money you have. Of course, people have always been aware of the spiritual challenges of earing and spending money, which is why many people throughout history have tried to renounce all material possessions: in an attempt to eliminate this challenge. However, no one can escape the challenge of needing food and shelter; we can only prove what we are willing to do to obtain our food and shelter.

Life would be less challenging if we didn't need to work for our food and shelter. But avoiding work only puts the burden of our consumption on someone else. It may only prove that we are willing to harm someone else's karma in an attempt to improve our own karma.

Vegans and vegetarians also can't evade the spiritual challenge of obtaining food and shelter because animal habitat still needs to be plowed under to grow their food and build their homes. In fact, a study by Cornell University in 2007 revealed that vegans and vegetarians actually require higher-quality animal habitat to be plowed under because fruits and vegetables must be grown in areas where the soil is fertile, whereas meat and dairy products from ruminant animals can be produced on lower-quality, pasture land.

Like the monks and nuns who cloister in their monastery to avoid all harmful activities, vegans and vegetarians also can't avoid the challenge of causing harm when sustaining themselves. They can only ask others to clear the land that they need for their farms, homes, roads, schools, stores, and so on. But does having someone else do the dirty-work absolve us?

Certainly, we should consume only what we need and we should all try to reduce our impact on the environment, but our need and impact cannot be zero. This is why every religion has struggled with asceticism and why most reject it: if we define our need too low, then we won't be living up to our full potential. Instead, we will just be proving that we are looking for a way out of life's challenges.

If it was only the impersonal wheel of karma that made life a challenge, then we might be able to avoid being challenged by extinguishing all desires, obtaining perfect karma, and entering Nirvana. But we can't extinguish all desires and obtain perfect karma as long as our bodies need food and shelter, so it's better to accept that God will always be challenging us to prove who we are by how we fulfill, or how we ask others to fulfill our body's needs.

Another challenge that many people want to eliminate is the inequities in wealth that result from our need for commerce. And the main way to supposedly eliminate the challenge of wealth inequality is socialism because, in a truly communal society, no one would be without an income and no one could gain excess wealth. Unfortunately, socialism hasn't eliminated wealth inequality because it can't eliminate the challenge of each citizen proving whether they are honest, tenacious, and compassionate enough to sustain a communal society.

Imperfect people cannot create perfect societies. Instead, our short-sighted and self-centered desires will always lead to challenging societies. Moreover, just the fact that everyone has differing desires, motivations, and abilities will lead to imperfect societies. And what does that ensure: it ensures that we will always be challenged by people with different incomes, abilities, and motivations, which ensures that we will always be forced to prove whether we are compassionate or cruel to those who are different from us.

Life is a constant challenge because everyone is different. Yet if the opposite were true and our genes, talents, and home environments were all exactly the same, then life would be a hollow world of mirrors.

Our world contains people who are both more talented and less talented than us, people who are both younger and older than us, and people who are both richer and poorer than us. These differences frustrate many people, yet a world where everyone was indistinguishable would be even more frustrating.

The opposite of life is not utopia; it's the empty nothingness that life was created from. This is the problem with all those religions that disparage life: the alternative to life is not Heaven or Nirvana; it's just empty space.

A world without any challenges where people weren't constantly proving who they were wouldn't have any meaning. To have meaning, everyone and everyday must present us with a different challenge and, thus, a different way of proving who we are.

Life's inequalities also cause many people to claim that, "Life is unfair." Yet this prophesy also can't be verified because there is no way to prove if God will reward or punish us in some future life. All we can know for sure is life is a constant challenge today because all unfairness isn't evened out in this world.

We can know "God's will" in so far as we can know the world that God maintains. Although many religions claim that the devil is ruining God's plans and that God needs us to implement his will, both of these beliefs imply that God is weak, which is illogical. What makes sense is that the world we live in today and the world that has existed throughout history is the world that God desires.

Although it's comforting to hear that the devil and not God is tempting us, if that were true, then the devil would have to be the creator of 99.9% of this world because the devil would have to create all the aspects of this world that challenge us. For example, the devil would have to create all the plants that are refined into all the drugs that tempt us and all the receptors in our brain that make those drugs so intoxicating. Yet there are also synthetic drugs that tempt us, so the devil would also have to be the creator of all the synthetic drugs and all their receptors as well. Furthermore, the devil would also have to be the creator of all the junk-foods that tempt us and all the taste-buds on our tongue that make those sugary, salty, and fatty foods so pleasurable. But many foods are unhealthy only when eaten in excess, so the devil would also have to be the creator of our desire to fill our stomach. Yet the desire to fill our stomach was a necessary impulse to build up fat for the lean times, which, thanks to modern science and agriculture, no longer come for most people.

In order for the devil to be responsible for all bad things, the devil would also have to be the creator of most of our impulses as well as most of our world. For example, the devil would have to be the creator of our impulse for anger, pride, dominance, laziness, jealously, and sex because these desires also challenge us and cause many people to prove some terrible things about themselves. But how much of the human body and how much of this world can we blame on the devil? Moreover, our impulses make sense when we see their evolutionary significance, so blaming the devil for our desires only makes it more difficult to understand and control what were once necessary urges.

Although the Book of Genesis tells us that God is the creator of all life, not all Christians want to accept that God created all the challenges in life. In fact, Pope Francis even suggested changing the two-thousand-year-old Lord's Prayer so it would no longer assert that "God leads us into temptation."

Genesis also tells us that "painful labor" is God's punishment for Adam listening to his wife. But if that prophesy were true, then we wouldn't be able to develop epidurals or machines to eliminate the pain of labor. Yet because we can triumph over life's challenges, there is little alternative but to accept that God created and wants us to overcome life's challenges.

Perhaps it would be easier to understand God's motivation for creating life's challenges if we considered the opposite scenario: the scenario where life wasn't a constant challenge. Perhaps we need to ask, "Why would God want us to live in the Garden of Eden or Nirvana where no one was challenged and, thus, no one was motivated to think?"

How would God maintain our universe if he wasn't constantly thinking? Perhaps this is why God constantly challenges us: he wants to be around other beings who are also constantly thinking. Unfortunately, most people don't want to think; most want to disengage, which is why so many people take drugs, seek mindless entertainment, and embrace simplistic religions.

The Western religions tell us that after the devil tricked Adam and Eve into eating the forbidden fruit, they covered themselves with fig leaves because they became aware that they were naked. But gaining self-awareness is how we reduce suffering and improve our lives, so how can we blame the devil for our self-awareness?

We are forced to constantly think because there are threats to our health all around us. There are drugs, junk foods, and sexually transmitted diseases in every society. There are also sharks in every ocean, poisonous insects around every home, and dangerous animals in every wilderness. Furthermore, there are psychopaths in every town, sociopaths in every workplace, and narcissists in every family. But instead of accepting that God put all these hazards into our world because he wants to keep our minds active and engaged, the major religions tell us that life's constant challenges are an error.

Most atheists assume that the universe is purely material and that God and our own consciousness are just illusions created by the material brain. In contrast, religious people should assume the opposite: that God and our consciousness are all that's real and that they create our sense of the material world.

If the universe exists only in the mind of God and, by transference, only in our mind, then we should place more emphasis on expanding our mind. We should assume that our awareness of the world is what creates the world and connects us to God.

We are not connected to the world by gravity; we are connected by our mind. That's why people who damage their mind through drug-use or idleness end up being disconnected from the world even though gravity still firmly binds their body to the Earth.

The more we learn about this world, the larger our world becomes. Conversely, the less we understand about this world, the smaller is our world. Moreover, because God is aware of everything, the more we become aware of, the more God will be able to relate to us. Yet because gaining knowledge takes time and energy and causes stress, many people turn away from learning and, thus, from what God wants us to do.

Too many religions cater to our desire to avoid the stress of thinking by telling us not to question. Too many religions tell their followers to scorn science and the media and avoid all knowledge outside the chosen religion. Too many reject God's seemingly obvious desire to expand our consciousness with their claim that we must silence our thoughts and just repeat a simple prayer or mantra.

Instead of acknowledging that God is pure consciousness who created this challenging world to make us think and expand our own consciousness, the Western religions claim that this world and our need to be aware of it is the result of Satan's trickery. In that sense, the Western religions are atheistic because they deny what God is doing.

The Eastern religions also overlook the purpose of life when they claim that life is suffering and that we should silence our thoughts and renounce the world. Although silencing one's mind through meditation is healthy in short, restful segments, if everyone emptied their mind and mediated all day like monks and nuns, then no one would have children and no one would tend the farm and the human race would disappear.

If humanity is to continue, then we must accept the mental, physical, emotional, and financial challenges of raising children. Furthermore, we must also accept the karmic challenges of farming even if growing fruits, grains, and vegetables is murder because dragging a plow across a field destroys the lives of all the creatures in that field.

Searching for a life devoid of physical, emotional, intellectual, and spiritual challenges is a natural reaction to living in a world filled with challenges. But if the human race is to survive, then we must all embrace the challenge of figuring out how 7.4 billion people and counting can exist on this planet without destroying the ecosystem because that will take a lot of thought and self-awareness from everyone.

Nirvana's "desire free" existence is similar to the Garden of Eden's "awareness free" existence because they are both the opposite of our present existence. This doesn't mean that humans didn't come from a state where we were all innocent and unaware, nor does it mean that some of us won't lose our awareness that we are male and female and return to this blank existence after death. But the quest to return to the unchallenging nothingness that life probably arose from is absurd. Moreover, the quest for an unthinking and desire-free existence only detracts from our daily lives where we are constantly struggling with dangers, desires, and imperfect choices.

Nothing about our challenging world indicates that God is preparing us for an afterlife where we don't have to think. If life's challenges prepare us for anything, it's more challenges.

Although an afterlife filled with challenges might seem stressful, a life without anything to do would be even more stressful. Again, this is why we invent games, pursue hobbies, and play sports: a life without challenges is unpleasant.

Chapter Eleven

Utopia

Although the major religions tell us that we are supposed to be living in Nirvana or the Garden of Eden, a life without any challenges would cause our mind, body, and spirit to atrophy. Perhaps this is why we have failed to create utopian societies here on Earth even though countless people have tried: God doesn't want our mind, body, and spirit to sit idle. Instead, God wants us to continually challenge us to learn and strive for a better world.

In order to create a truly carefree society, we would have to design autonomous machines to run the world or we would have to find perfect people to run the world. But it's doubtful if any rational person believes that we can build self-governing robots or find perfect leaders to create a completely carefree society. Of course, this is why so many people look to magical occurrences, like a messiah or a harmonic convergence: because most people know that humans can't create a perfect world.

Although we have continually failed to create perfect societies, many people still claim that a purely capitalist ideology or a purely socialist ideology will lead to the perfect world. But if that were true, then some nation would have created a fair and stable capitalistic society or a fair and stable socialistic society by now. Yet history has continually shown that neither society is stable or fair. Instead, the only societies that endure are those with a constantly fluctuating mixture of socialism and capitalism, so this must be the society that God wants even if this erratic, hybrid society constantly challenges us.

Although it seems like someone should be smart enough to devise the perfect government, the government is not a machine. The government is just a collection of people, so the real challenge is to inspire or control large groups of people so that no malfeasance goes on. But how can we inspire or control millions of individuals so that no bad behavior occurs?

Obviously, all of our religions and political ideologies have failed to inspire people to push aside their unhealthy impulses. This is why we hire police: in an attempt to force people to behave properly. Unfortunately, it's impossible to police every potential wrongdoer. Moreover, because the police are also human, we need police to police the police. But who will police the police who police the police?

Although the different branches of our government are supposed to police each other, there is no guarantee that the people who control the different branches of government won't become corrupt and collude against the taxpayers. There is also no guarantee that the leaders of industry won't collude and just pretend to be in competition with each other. Yet we argue about the problems in government and industry as if these institutions were just giant machines that only needed the proper software. As if some ideology from the left or some ideology from the right could force everyone in government and industry to be honest, diligent, and conscientious. As if we could create a utopian society where everyone was forced to behave properly and God no longer needed to challenge us and make us to prove who we are.

It appears that God will always be challenging us and society will always need laws, police, and prisons because many people will always seek the path of least resistance. That's why our hopes must not be pinned on Utopia, but on coping with people who are constantly challenged and constantly proving if they are able to abide by their honorable and healthy motivations.

Our inability to stop crime and God's unwillingness to clearly punish criminals is distressing because most of us want to live in a world free of crime. It's distressing because we constantly see and hear about blue and white-collar crime and we would like karma, the messiah, or the government to stop all these crimes. But the messiah hasn't shown up, karma doesn't stop crime, and our government can't prevent all crimes, so God must want us to be free to commit crimes. Perhaps God wants to see who is willing to control their criminal impulses and who is willing to do something about all the crimes they see and hear about.

If we can accept that God doesn't want us to solve all this world's problems and be done with it, then we can stop waiting for the messiah, a harmonic convergence, or some political ideology to create the perfect world. We might even start planning for the world that has always existed and probably will always exist: a world where every person in every generation is forced to grow up and prove whether they will be a part of, or an obstacle to a decent society.

It's frustrating that the health of society is ultimately dependent on each person's desire to be healthy, honest, and compassionate because we all know how impulsive, self-centered, and self-destructive people can be. It's frustrating because if even one person proves themselves to be lazy, cruel, greedy, dishonest, cowardly, or self-destructive, then society breaks down by that much. It's distressing because billions of people are proving themselves to be lazy, cruel, greedy, dishonest, cowardly, and self-destructive and we would like to stop all this free will and personal responsibility. We would like God, karma, a harmonic convergence, or the government to force everyone to be honest, healthy, and compassionate. But free will and bad behaviors continue to exist, so God must like challenging us even if many people prove some terrible things about themselves.

Life is a challenge because God allows us to make our own decisions, many of which are bad decisions. To put it another way, life is a challenge because God gives us free will. But in the Utopia where God, karma, or the government takes away our ability to choose our behavior, life would be far worse.

God gives us free will to take advantage other people by not immediately punishing us. We are even free to molest children because child molesters often elude law enforcement and because child molesters obviously aren't stopped by karma or God. Many people feel that this proves "might makes right." But it may only prove that we have free will, which means that we have the freedom to harm others.

God may not like or favor the victors; he may just allow everyone to prove which side they favor. And if more people favor the corrupt, then they will win.

Throughout history, millions of honest people have been destroyed by mobs and crooked institutions. Does this prove that God likes dishonest people? Perhaps atheists are correct that the existence of tyrants proves that God doesn't exist. Or maybe it shows that God wants good behavior to be a challenge.

God, evolution, or the laws of physics have made it more challenging to be honest, healthy, and compassionate than to be dishonest, unhealthy, and selfish. Does this prove that God favors the baser elements in human nature, or could it mean that God wants good behavior to be an accomplishment and bad behavior to be no challenge at all? Could it mean that when God sees good behavior, he wants to know that this behavior didn't arise by accident because good behavior requires conscious and sustained effort?

God not only allows us to steal, cheat, and abuse others, but God actually makes these selfish behaviors easier than honest and compassionate behaviors. This may seem odd and unfair. But how could we have free will if we lacked the ability to do bad things? Moreover, why would God admire good behavior if everyone was forced to be good or if good behavior came easily, naturally, and instinctively?

We are free to take advantage of the weak and we are free to ignore the crimes we see around us. Yet we are also free to counter the bullies and stop the criminals. We are free to be selfish and indifferent, or compassionate and heroic because God doesn't clearly reward one or clearly punish the others. However, it's clear that we prove who we are by which person we choose to be.

It's frustrating that we don't know if God will reward or punish us for the things we prove about ourselves. But, as with every other one of life's "flaws," this is just another reason why life is a challenge and why we are constantly proving who we are: we aren't certain if our actions will be rewarded, punished, or forgiven.

If we were certain our good deeds would be rewarded and our selfishness would be punished, then life wouldn't be a challenge. But we aren't certain if our actions will be rewarded, punished, or forgiven, and this challenges us and forces us to prove what's in our heart. It forces everyone to think and struggle with their conscience before they act, even if it's only a brief struggle for most people.

Although many people speculate about how the laws of physics might give us free will, what truly gives us free will is our uncertainty about God's existence and our uncertainty about whether God will punish, reward, or forgive us for the things we do. For no one thinks about quantum mechanics before they act; what we think about is whether God or karma exists and what they will do about our good or bad behavior.

Our uncertainty about the existence of God and karma and our uncertainty about how God or karma will respond to our behavior is what truly gives us free will. Yet even though most religions claim that free will is real, most religions also claim to know exactly how, why, and when God will punish, reward, or forgive us. However, no matter how much faith we proclaim to have, we are all uncertain and, thus, we are all freely choosing our behavior. We are all choosing without divine coercion whether to be a villain, a saint, or something in between.

No one in their right mind would be a tyrant if they were certain of divine punishment. But uncertainty also allows for virtue because no one could be called virtuous if they were certain that a reward would be given for each of their sacrifices. Yet how many religions teach that uncertainty is necessary for virtue? Again, don't most religions claim to know exactly which behaviors will secure God's reward?

Although most religions and even many atheists struggle to explain why bad things happen to good people, it should be obvious that if good things always happened to good people and bad things always happened to bad people, then life wouldn't be a challenge. Yet the obvious isn't accepted because most religious people and even many atheists can't believe that an all-powerful and loving God would challenge them and make them prove who they are. As if a benevolent God would only indulge us and never challenge or judge us.

It appears that the laws of this world must pass an emotional litmustest before they are accepted. It appears that many, if not most people feel that they can ignore any law they don't like. As if we could reject Galileo, Darwin, and the fact that every aspect of this world was designed to challenge us and make us prove who we are because we don't want such an exasperating world. Unfortunately, the world exists independent of our desires, so we must objectively study and accept what exists.

Chapter Twelve

Aging

Another fundamental reason why life is a constant challenge is because everyone is continually growing older. And, as with all of life's other challenges, the Eastern religions see aging as a flaw while the Western religions see aging as punishment brought about by the devil instead of accepting that the aging process was purposely designed by God so everyone would be constantly challenged throughout their life.

Aging makes life a continual challenge because the old and wise are continually replaced by a new and untested generation. In essence, life is a continual challenge because God, or the laws of physics make us grow older at the same rate we grow wiser. This ensures that each person will have only enough time to prove who they are before they must move on.

Science doesn't fully understand why we age. But philosophically it's easy to see why God would want us to age: life wouldn't be a challenge to an immortal being. Immortals could ignore every challenge and they would never prove who they are because they would always have more time to prove something else. Yet we have only a limited amount of time to meet life's challenges and prove who we are.

Immortality may seem like the ideal state because immortals would always be young and able to redo anything they did. But being able to redo all your actions would make your actions fleeting and meaningless. In contrast, our actions are eternal and meaningful because everyone we interact with is growing older.

Our actions are important because we grow old, because our friends, relatives, co-worker, and neighbors grow old, and because we can't take people back in time to redo our actions. This is why it's difficult to believe that science will ever vanquish the aging process: it's to believe that scientists could remove the challenge, meaning, and consequences from our actions.

Certainly, science has extended our lifespan, but it's more of an extension of old age than a renewal of our youth. To make the passage of time unchallenging and unimportant, scientists would have to be able to turn adults into teens or preteens again.

For the foreseeable future, life will be a "timed test" where our actions and choices are final. That's frustrating. But ignoring the spiritual need for aging only leads to more frustration.

Both the Eastern and Western religions struggle to make sense of aging and provide some comfort to those who are old. But aging shouldn't be depicted as punishment or as the earthly cause of suffering because this neglects all the meaning that aging creates in our life.

Because aging is necessary to give our actions meaning and to make life a challenge, our religions should explain how the aging process was perfectly designed by God so that everyone would be constantly challenged throughout their life.

Perhaps the major religions would focus more on the spiritual need, the spiritual purpose, and the spiritual challenge of aging if they focused more on young people than the elderly. Unfortunately, most religions profit mainly from comforting those who are old and tired of aging.

We need two separate religions: one for the young and one for the elderly because young people shouldn't be subjected to their parents and grandparents' disillusionment with life. Young people should be taught about the joys of life, and not that this world is flawed, they are sinners, and they should renounce their earthly desires. Young people should be taught about all the challenges that they will encounter in this world so they can always prove the best things about themselves.

Perhaps one religion could help young people understand, enjoy, and improve this world, while the other religion helps the elderly move beyond their fading desires, their regrets, and this impermanent world. Perhaps the constant disparaging of this world would end if our religions would focus more on helping young people understand the life that stretches out before them than on helping the elderly turn away from the life that lies behind them.

Again, we can know God's will in so far as we can know the world that God maintains. Moreover, our religions could unite us by explaining this world and all its challenges. But most religions cater primarily to those who are looking for a way out of this world, so they tell us about Heaven and Nirvana, or worlds where there won't be any challenges.

Most religions are just a lament about the paradise we lost as we grew old. And growing old is something to lament about. Nevertheless, this constant disparaging of life by the world's religions just keeps adults from remembering that Planet Earth is still a paradise to the young, which makes it even more difficult for young people to understand, enjoy, and improve this world.

Although it's comforting for the elderly to think about the end times and the afterlife, young people should be thinking only about their future times and all the things they will do in this life. Moreover, although many elderly people see life as suffering, young people should only see life as fun and joyful.

As adults, we must make sure that children don't see life as suffering and aren't wishing for the world's end. Hopefully, we can create a world where children are unable to grasp why such themes even exist in religion until they also grow old.

Our religions shouldn't vilify this world. They should explain why our world is as it is, as it seems to have always been, and as it will probably always be: a challenge that forces everyone to prove who they are.

If we want our desires to be fulfilled, the we must desire what actually exists. We must desire a world where everyone is constantly challenged, even if we are often challenged in an unpleasant way and even if we are often forced to challenge some unpleasant people. We must also desire a world where everyone constantly proves who they are, even if many people prove some terrible things about themselves.

To enjoy life and to help young people create a better world, we must find religious and philosophical beliefs that we can all verify, agree on, and plan for. For even if the laws of this world initially challenge us, our life will be better when we know what the future will bring us.

♦ ♦ ♦

Index

Made in the USA
Las Vegas, NV
05 April 2024